From a Child Soldier

*The journey of turning scars to a star –
A true life story*

MIX
Papier aus verantwortungsvollen Quellen
Paper from responsible sources
FSC® C105338

The Author Ishmeal Alfred Charles

Ishmeal Alfred Charles

From a Child Soldier to a humanitarian

The journey of turning scars to a star

A true life story

Dear Team at MACS,

Delighted about the walk you do. I am pleased to be connected.

Happy Reading!.

Charles

Bibliographic information from the German National Library The German National Library lists this publication in the German National Bibliography; Detailed bibliographic data is available on the Internet at http://dnb.d-nb.de.

Imprint:
ISBN-13: 9783757886042
© 2022–2023 Ishmeal Alfred Charles, all rights reserved.
Photo: © Infinity Studios
Graphics: © Esther Mattar from New Salone Woman Design Limited, https://www.facebook.com/NewSaloneWomanDesign
Layout: Daniela Brotsack, www.exlibris-d.de
Manufacturing and Publishing: BoD - Books on Demand, Norderstedt

*Eclipsing the odd:
from child soldier to humanitarian actor,
the life story of a determined boy
who became a man of service*

Ishmeal Alfred Charles

Chapter I

Humble Beginnings

I am Ishmael Alfred Charles, born on April 14th, 1983, in Sierra Leone during the Easter celebrations. It was in Freetown, the capital city of the country once referred to as the "Athens of West Africa". My parents were Abu Alfred Charles, hailing from Torwama, a community located in Bo District, Southern Sierra Leone, and Aminata Yomie Tejan from Freetown. Sadly, both have passed away.

My father was born to Catholic parents and was the second child out of two. However, at a very tender age, fate led my father to grow up without the love of his father (my grandfather), who succumbed to death due to some ailments. Additionally, my paternal grandmother died soon after my father's birth.

Following the death of his parents, my father's only option was to live with his elder brother, Uncle Joseph. Uncle Joseph had a daughter named Theresa, and both lived first in Bo and later in Freetown.

It was difficult to tell the age difference between my father and his niece, as they were often seen doing almost everything together. Their affection for each other could be compared to that of two identical twins, with one cap fitting both. From dawn till dusk, they were always seen together, tending to the tasks that each day presented, including looking after Theresa's siblings.

Their care for each other continued for years until physical and biological maturity set in. This brought about changes and balances. By then, my father had started making friends extensively and was often playing soccer with his peers in the locality. Football, or soccer, brought immense joy to these two friends.

My father shone like a „shining marble" on the soccer field and was admired by many. As his fame grew like a volcanic eruption, soccer took him from one community to another. Those who witnessed my father's play still tell me that he was a force to be reckoned with when it came to excellent dribbling skills, particularly in the midfield area.

At the age of 18, my father became a masterpiece in the art of soccer. His fame was said to outshine his physical stature. Ishmael Kondeh was my father's best buddy on and off the pitch. Both were said to be exemplary on the football field, and hardly any match they played was not won in their favor. I called them "the Fantastic Two".

Legends have it that even those who were not soccer fans fell for their footwork on the football field. As their fame spread, my father and his friend toured the length and breadth of Sierra Leone, playing the country's most cherished sport – soccer. The duo played for larger communities and non-division football teams.

Years rolled on, and by the age of 20, my father was known nationwide. This drew the attention of larger football clubs. Eastern Lions Football Club, undoubtedly one of the best teams in the country, secured the services of my father and his playmate.

During a particular Christmas period, my father and his playmate traveled with Eastern Lions to Kono District to participate in a month-long tournament. It was an exciting opportunity as they had always wanted to explore Kono, which is known for having one of the world's finest deposits of diamonds.

However, my father's impression of Kono upon seeing it was quite the opposite of what he had imagined. The district, despite its beautiful deposits, turned out to be extremely underdeveloped. It was quite a disappointment for my father, who had envisioned a well-developed district due to the mining activities. Kono District, even with its valuable resources, always reminded him of Ziggy Marley's song with the line "living in the diamond city with a broken heart."

Nonetheless, the deplorable state of Kono didn't deter my father from showcasing his remarkable dribbling skills. The people of Kono nodded in approval of his unique qualities. By the end of the tournament, my father had made acquaintances. One memory that always crossed his mind was the hospitality of the indigenous people.

Kono became a melting pot for my father. He reunited with old friends from various leagues he had played in and made many new friends as well. The tournament ended with Eastern Lions FC defeating Diamond Stars FC (of Kono) with a score of four goals to two (4-2). His team was paraded through the principal streets of Kono in Koidu City. To this day, some who witnessed the grand finale still recount the tale of my father's excellent dribbling skills. He was "the perfect guy for the perfect moment."

After Eastern Lions' success in Kono, the team decided to stay for a week, unaware that his „shining stars" would never return to Freetown. The duo (my father and Ishmael Kondeh) harbored a plan to prolong their stay in Kono, especially since Ishmael Kondeh's family resided in a township called Yormandu.

Exploring the diamond mines in Koidu City became another secret endeavor of my father and Ishmael Kondeh. Koidu City was the heart of diamond mining, attracting youth from all over the nation in search of fortune, as well as international investors. This rush to Kono for mineral exploration played a role in the country's brutal civil war that lasted for eleven years.

There was no age limit for engaging in these activities, and even children took part in illegal mining. My father and his friend seized the opportunity. Sadly, the Eastern Lions coach couldn't persuade his best players to return with him. With a heavy heart, he departed for Freetown.

Despite being captivated by the prospects of quick wealth, my father and Ishmael Kondeh never lost sight of soccer. Local coaches sought their expertise, and soon they were playing for local teams. These two inseparable friends continued to chase their dream of greatness on the field, aiming to play overseas someday. However, this dream was never realized due to the allure of Kono's diamonds, which ultimately ended their hopes for international stardom.

My mother, on the other hand, was born to parents of Yoruba origin with Krio Language as their lingua franca. History holds that the "Yorubas" were from Nigeria, a country located in West Africa. My maternal grandparents are also linked with the "Akus/Fourah Bays/Frobay" and were descendants of recaptive slaves liberated during the colonial era by the British Naval Patrol on the high waters of Sierra Leone. Upon their liberation, they settled in Freetown as freed slaves together with another batch of freed slaves from Nova Scotia, Canada.

As these freed slaves settled in Freetown, religious tolerance and communal practices were the order of the day. The freed slaves from Nova Scotia were mostly Christians, and the Akus/Fourah Bays were mostly Muslims. The Akus were dubbed as "Muslim Krio," and this was so because the "Krios" have a typical identity similar to people in Europe or the United States of America – their attitude, dress code, language, and accent speak volumes about the Krios. Names given to

Krio children have a blend of both English and African (Yoruba) elements.

To this date, the Akus/Fourah Bays are settled in the Fourah Bay Community situated in the east-end of Freetown, very close to the central business area of the city and Queen Elizabeth II Quay – the third natural harbor in the world, named after Her Majesty, Queen Elizabeth II, during her visit to Sierra Leone in 1961, a year that also marked the country's independence on April 27th.

The Fourah Bay Community also boasts the very first college in West Africa – Fourah Bay College (FBC), founded in 1827. The college's exceptional academic performance attracted students from far and wide. Sierra Leone became a hub for academia in Africa, earning the country the moniker „Athens of West Africa."

My maternal grandfather was a foreman in the Sierra Leone Government Railway in the late 1940s. He was among the first Africans to hold such a prestigious position at that time. His service at the railway led him to move from place to place, and he was also engaged in trading activities involving farm products. He was a developmentally-oriented individual, and through his hard work, he built houses in the Wellington Community, also located in the east-end of Freetown, and in Baoya, a township in the Moyamba District, South of Sierra Leone.

Grandpa was a full-blown polygamous man, but my grandma happened to be his precious gem. He was moved by my grandma's dedication to hard work, and she often bailed him out when he faced financial difficulties. Her profits from small-scale businesses were instrumental in financially supporting my grandpa. Posterity remembers my grandma as a virtuous woman who stood firm to ensure her loving husband's success at all costs.

Grandpa was not a perfect human, but he was a devoted Muslim, and his good deeds in the Islamic community are still remembered. His home was a safe haven for the vulnerable. While he rarely spoke on public platforms, when he did, his words carried weight. Grandpa exhibited love and care towards his children, and he welcomed discussions with potential suitors who sought his daughters' hands in marriage. He refrained from choosing husbands for his daughters; instead, the decision of choosing the right suitor rested with his daughters themselves. Among his five daughters, my mother was the „apple of his eye."

My mother followed in her mother's footsteps when it came to trade. She was deeply engrossed in business to the extent that she hardly had time for marriage. She traded in foodstuffs, including coconut, sugar, and peppermint. My sweet mama was persuasive with her customers, and she had the unique habit of communicating with them in a language they understood best.

Allow me to vividly describe my mother. She was born a twin but lost her twin shortly after birth. Growing up, she never indulged in trivial conversations, and her peers and community members nicknamed her „Big Woman." A quick learner, she mastered six local languages: Mende, Temne, Soso, Fullah, Madingo, and Bambara, a Malian dialect. While her formal education was limited, she possessed exceptional business skills that attracted customers from far and wide. Business was thriving in Freetown until fate steered her toward a new direction in life.

At the request of Aunty Nafi, her cherished elder sister, she left for Kono. Aunty Nafi had married and resettled in Kono with her husband. She pleaded with my grandpa and the family to allow my mother to accompany her. This decision marked the beginning of a new chapter in my mother's early adult life.

During this time, my father remained in Kono, deeply committed to his football aspirations and exploring mining sites in search of fortune. Music served as his emotional refuge, providing motivation and solace during tough times. My dad's heart belonged to reggae and blues music. He immersed himself in songs by artists such as Bob Nesto Marley, Eric Donaldson, Joseph Hills (Joe Hills), Alpha Blonde, Peter Tosh, Jimmy Cliff, Tracy Chapman, and many more.

His passion for music drove him to memorize the songs of his reggae and blues icons. He openly danced and sang along to their tunes. In contrast, my mother wasn't easily swayed by music's allure and found little pleasure in clubs and dancehalls. She had a fondness for staged dramas (concerts) and comedy. Among the comedy groups she cherished, „The Professionals" stood out. This group featured performers like Dan Dogo, Baynkutay, and Lord Bongo, who frequently appeared in soap opera radio dramas across the country, consistently bringing laughter to my mother.

Half a year swiftly passed in Kono, during which my mother formed close friendships. Aunty Mboyo (M'bor) was her closest friend, and they took turns braiding each other's hair on weekends in their respective homes. Aunty Mboyo lived a few blocks away from the Kondeh residence, a sizable compound where my father lived. According to eyewitness accounts, my father was deeply smitten with my mother. He would sneak to catch glimpses of her when she came to visit her friend, although he lacked the courage to directly express his feelings to her.

Evidently, love was in the air – a palpable sentiment sensed everywhere. On a fateful evening, my father and his friend Ishmeal were returning home after a soccer game when he saw my mother. This time, the shy guy summoned the courage to propose his love to her. My mother was moved by the genuine affection of the young man, and before long, they fell deeply in love. In my wildest imagination, I can only describe their enchanting encounter as a „fairy tale destined for a happy ending." The lovebirds dated, married, and within five years, they welcomed their first son, named Ibrahim. My elder brother was followed by my late sister, Memuna, and five years later, I entered the world.

I can genuinely say that my birth brought a stroke of luck for my father. A few hours after I was born, my dad struck a fortunate find – one of the finest diamonds that momentarily lifted our family's fortunes. Remarkably, at that juncture, my parents were on the brink of divorcing.

Growing up, the moments I had with my mother were the very best of my life. As a child born into a typical cultured African family, I was always awakened from my bed by my mother very early in the morning as the cock crowed. My mother always knew how to get things done her way. I can still recall the charming names she used to get me out of bed in order to brush my teeth and take my bath – "sweet darling, fatfut lip, daddy …"

Around age three, I used to be an interesting crier. When my mother was dressed to go out, mostly to the city center to buy her marketing goods, I would ask her if I could go with her, and she would reject me, telling me to go and sit. I would tell her that I would cry, and she would spread a mat for me to sit on if I wanted to cry. I would indeed sit and cry for hours until she returned, and I would then ask her, „Are you back? Can I stop crying now?" She would answer, „Yes, stop crying now, please." Then I would stop crying. This is something my aunts still laugh at me about.

At age 6, I had mastered the art of waking up early, and it was all fun doing things without being pampered. I only came to understand the importance of her wake-up calls when I was much older. I can proudly say that I had the best mother in the whole wide world. Every piece of advice she gave me is worth a lot to me today in my social and personal life.

Another moment from my childhood that always crosses my mind is the time when I was learning to read and write. As with most kids, you always start with the basics (ABC…, 1, 2, 3…). Learning at that age in my typical family setting that involved an elder brother, Ibrahim, to guide my schoolwork was truly a difficult moment for me. My parents always had to compel my elder brother to practically hold my hand so that I could learn to write properly. Ibrahim was very strict with me, and I could barely escape the learning session without receiving a couple of knocks or slaps on my hand, especially on account of him being right-handed and me being left-handed. He always compelled me to write with my right hand, and in the process, I did receive some scoldings.

In my humble beginnings and for most of my life, I could not enjoy the love and bond with my father enough. When I was only 9 years old, divorce came knocking, and out of mutual consent, my mum and dad divorced. The divorce led my mother to relocate to Freetown with three kids to feed. It was a burden on a poor boy like me to part with my father's love.

After the divorce, word reached my mother that my father had remarried, and within a short period of time, my father cut off the remittances he had been sending to us. Psychologically, I was deeply affected because I loved seeing my father around. News again reached us that my father had relocated to some other faraway place. There were moments when I would burst out in tears because I could neither see nor locate my father. What I always did to capture my father in my mind's eye was to listen to the song "Remember Me," by Lucky Dube, the late South African reggae legend. The emotionally charged lyrics by Lucky Dube depicted a lost father who had gone to a faraway land, leaving behind his wife and kids – such was my similar situation.

Interestingly, the divorce gave my mother a new lease on life to move forward. She never folded her arms and cried over my father's departure. She became more determined to take care of us, as she was now a single parent. I remember coming home from school, sobbing because I was bullied by my peers over a football match. I thought my mum, like most African women, would get up, tidy her dress, and go after the kids, but she never did that. She told me not to mind the kids because I was far better than them and destined for great things. She took me in her arms, wiped away my tears, and tickled my cheeks until I laughed. Years later, I realized that most of the kids who bullied me back then are neither found nor counted among the successful.

Despite the rough times, my mum stood firm in ensuring that we did not beg from other kids or neighbors. I compare my mum's struggle to raise us to Buchi Emecheta's novel, "The Joys of Motherhood," which depicts the struggles a mother goes through to raise her children amidst a male chauvinistic society. In spite of the challenging times, my mum stood firm in ensuring that we did not beg from other kids or neighbors.

I do recall my physical appearance back then as a child growing up. I would often grumble to my mum that I was too skinny to fit into outfits, and my mother would just smile and say, "My son, this is exactly how I looked at your age." As a kid hearing such words from my mother, I found it very difficult to believe, especially when looking at her physical structure. I have come to realize now that among all her children, we look very much alike, especially now that I have grown up and lost that skinny appearance. Interestingly, members of my family and others who knew my mother in life tell me that my smile always reminds them of my mother.

Today, I reminisce about my mother's resilient attributes in raising me, and such attributes have become my mantra as I strive to create a positive impact in the lives of people, especially the less privileged. She was the kind of woman who never bowed down to pressure or challenges. She will always remain „the darling of my heart."

CHAPTER 2

The Rising Tide

One of my primary school teachers used to say, „Education is the key to success." In everything you do, whether formal or informal, education is always the necessity needed for success. My early primary education was indeed interesting. Thank goodness for school and the overwhelming effect of imparting knowledge, confidence, and esteem. I sometimes wonder how my life would have been without education.

Memories of my school days are like two sides of a coin; you could find happiness on one side and sadness on the other side. Back in my pre-school days which I spent at Bush and Town Pre-School, located in Wellington Community, Aunty Kaynama was my teacher, and she was like a mother to me. She helped establish the blueprint of my academic career.

As a kid in kindergarten, it was hard to distinguish between good and evil. Aunty Kaynama was there to be the guardian angel and she helped shape the lives of most kids back then. She had a spectacular way of telling stories from the Holy Bible and a book called „My Book of Bible Stories" that would capture your complete attention, making the classroom very quiet.

Aunty Kaynama was truly a guardian angel who eradicated evil thoughts from our hearts and ensured that as kids, we prioritized education above all things. I can proudly boast that the moral lessons from „My Book of Bible Stories" were instrumental. She was also a disciplinarian who made it a duty for the pupils to take their school work very seriously. I can wholeheartedly tell you that the moral lessons I learned from Aunty Kaynaman became the driving force behind my humanitarian work today.

My first experiences with humanitarian work occurred during my primary school days at Saint Edward's Primary School in Freetown, where I was part of the Cubs Scout Society and also volunteered for the Red Cross Society. Due to my involvement in some of these humanitarian activities, I began to appreciate humanity more and more, nurturing the notion of giving my very best to the service of humanity, especially to those in dire situations like the homeless, orphans, and victims of war and natural disasters.

At an early age, I was also nurtured on the path of quality education. I can still remember my father's words, especially when I needed something from him. He would always say, „Just make good grades, and I will make you happy." Additionally, he would always tell me to write a Letter of Request, even for the simplest needs. With this guidance, I was made to work very hard. Though it was a challenge for a boy of age 9, considering the grammatical errors, subject-verb agreement, and the like, it actually improved my letter writing and composition skills.

My primary school days were very challenging. But thank God for Aunty Kaynama, who had earlier planted a seed of resilience and hard work. As I mentioned earlier, my primary days marked the period of separation between my father and mother. My mother was staying in Freetown while my father was in Kono. Due to this distance, I always spent holidays in Kono with my father at the end of the school year. My father loved me dearly, and after the holidays, I could not return to Freetown to continue the next academic year. Therefore, I gained admission at the United Methodist Church (UMC) Primary School in Koidu City and also at Ahmadiyya Primary School in Yormandu, Sandor Chiefdom, all in Kono District and in subsequent holidays.

In a nutshell, I can tell you that I finally had stable schooling when I was in Class 5, enrolled at Saint Edward's Primary School in Freetown, and by then, I was residing with my paternal uncle and his wife.

Finally, I had a stable primary education when I was in Class 5, attending the Saint Edward's Primary School, and by then, I was with my paternal uncle and his wife. Memories of this household always bring me to tears. Living with my uncle was very hard, and I had to do almost every household chore at that age. Cooking became a must, and I learned to cook right there. I was given a small amount as lunch money for school, and luckily, I had a friend named Harding who was always willing to share his food with me, but not without a price. In order to have some of Harding's delicious fries, I had to exchange my lunch money of Le150. Nowadays, there is hardly anything that you can buy with such an amount of money in Sierra Leone. Harding's fries gave me the sustenance I needed in class, allowing me to concentrate fully.

Most pupils attending Saint Edward's Primary School choose Saint Edward's Secondary School as their preferred secondary school after completing the National Primary School Examination (NPSE). Both schools belong to the same Catholic Mission. I was planning to do the same, but there was a Saint Edward's Secondary School teacher by the name of Mr. Smith who totally discouraged me from choosing Saint Edward's Secondary as my school of choice.

Mr. Smith resided in the same house as my uncle, and I was often terrified by his actions due to his love for corporal punishment. He frequently boasted about punishing students, which frightened me. As a result, I opted for another secondary school, the Prince of Wales School. I remember when I was given the School of Choice Form to fill out; I dared not show the form to my uncle because Mr. Smith might persuade him to have me attend Saint Edward's Secondary School. Thus, I had no option but to fill out the form quietly in my room.

I finally took the NPSE in 1996 and scored an aggregate of 321, which made me eligible to attend any secondary school across the country. Choosing the Prince of Wales School was one of the best decisions I have ever made in my life.

I owe the success of my basic education to Aunty Kaynama, who laid the foundation of my education; and also, to Mrs. Josephine Cole and Mr. Samuel Charles, both of whom taught me at Saint Edward's Primary School. Mr. Samuel Charles, in particular, taught me in Class 6 and was very fond of me for being intelligent and obedient in class, as well as for sharing the same last name as him. He often joked in class that those with the surname "Charles" are very serious and would never be losers in life.

One of the most memorable moments was one of the motivational stories told by Mr. Charles. He once recounted a story about a tortoise that refused to give up despite facing challenges. The story highlighted how the tortoise was ridiculed and insulted, but it persevered and won the race in the end. I've always associated my journey to success with the story of the persevering tortoise.

Chapter 3

Eclipsing the Odds

My homeland, Sierra Leone, could be referred to in many ways, but one standout characteristic is that my country is known as the „home of the free and the brave." Sierra Leone boasts a rich history of cultural diversity and is renowned for being the birthplace of quality education in West Africa, and by extension, Africa.

The tiny West African nation derived its name from a Portuguese sailor named Pedro Da Cintra, who arrived in Sierra Leone in 1462 during the rainy season. He was awestruck by the noisy yet beautiful display of lightning and thunderous blasts he witnessed from his fleet stationed on the cape of the Atlantic Ocean. The hills on the outskirts of Freetown, resembling a „sitting lion," gave Da Cintra and his crew the impression that led to the name „Sierra Loya," meaning ‚Lion Mountain' in Portuguese. Even though lions are rare in Sierra Leone, the Portuguese associated the thunder with the roars of lions echoing through the stunning mountains.

I can assure you that Sierra Leone is the best place to be. One thing is certain: the foundation for modern education in the West African sub-region was laid in Sierra Leone. My country stood as the envy of other nations in terms of academic achievements across West Africa and beyond, both during and after the colonial era. Speaking of the people of my country always brings smiles to those who have visited. Sierra Leone, often affectionately called „Sweet Mama Salone," is not only rich in minerals but also in cultural diversity. Religious tolerance is a fundamental principle, evident in communal responsibilities and inter-religious marriages between Christians and Muslims. Despite bearing the scars of an 11-year brutal war, the memories of which still linger in the streets, Sierra Leone persists.

I was born long before the brutal war erupted. While life was challenging back then, it couldn't be compared to the horrors of the war. Prior to the war, my family had our own little world. Even in the midst of my parents' divorce, as children, we found security amid the winds of revolution that signaled the impending outbreak of one of Africa's deadliest conflicts. As with all wars, the toll was immense: thousands killed, thousands displaced or turned into refugees, thousands subjected to amputation, women and girls subjected to rape, government institutions and homes reduced to ashes, and children conscripted by rebels.

These catastrophes unfolded during the 11-year civil war, masquerading as a regime change effort. The Revolutionary United Front (RUF), led by Foday Saybana Sankoh, an army of disaffected individuals, aimed to overthrow the governing All Peoples' Congress (APC Government) led by President Joseph Saidu Momoh. Many Sierra Leoneans initially agreed with the RUF's stance against the corrupt APC administration, discriminatory appointments, and the stifling of opposition voices, believed to be influenced by former Head of State, Siaka Probyn Steven. It was against this backdrop that the RUF emerged, initially driven by the goal of rectifying these issues. Personally, I never anticipated that this deadly war would penetrate our small family world. Sadly, I was proven entirely wrong.

On 23 March 1991, the war erupted in Bomaru, Kailahun District, East of Sierra Leone, and the RUF began conquering and gaining territories. The war, which had initially started on a promising course, turned against the citizenry it was meant to protect.

I was 8 years old when the Revolutionary United Front (RUF) rebels began attacking and taking over villages. The capital, Freetown, was quite far from the rebel attacks' location, and no one anticipated their reach to the city. Freetown served as a hub where people from diverse ethnic, cultural, religious, and economic backgrounds lived. The residents were unaware that the capital would become the center of the war. It's safe to say that Freetown acted as a ‚melting pot' for various opinions, and no single ethnic group dominated over the others. Before the insurgency, the capital was a peaceful place to live with a population of 3 to 4 million.

It all began in 1991 when my mother sent me on holiday to my father in Kono, where he worked in the diamond mines. Holidays were highly anticipated by kids in Sierra Leone, especially after a challenging academic year. On that significant day, my mother packed my bag with clothes and school books, escorted me to the bus station, handed me over to the bus driver, and bid me goodbye. This marked the start of an adventurous journey for a 9-year-old boy heading to what would become a heavily impacted zone behind enemy lines. Like other kids my age, I had no idea about the challenges that lay ahead.

My joyful dreams of a delightful holiday were abruptly interrupted a few days after I arrived in Kono. One cool and windy morning, a regiment of RUF rebels surprised us by capturing the diamond-rich area of Kono. As a strategically valuable region with diamonds and other minerals, the rebels sought to fuel their emerging ambitions. Their aim was to swiftly transform this habitable and prosperous diamond-bearing area into a battleground of despair, ruin, and bitter memories.

Everyone was caught off-guard as the sound of gunshots and rocket-propelled grenades echoed. The air filled with smoke and dust, obscuring the crimson hues of the twilight sky. It felt like an ugly nightmare, yet I knew it was all too real. I looked around, searching for my friends with whom I had been playing with a makeshift football, but they were nowhere to be seen.

The atmosphere turned chaotic as people scattered in all directions, accompanied by the frightened cries of children and toddlers. The rhythm of their (the rebels') deadly AK-47s (Kalashnikovs) blended with the terrified whispers of adults and children. Amidst the dust that made everything appear like a nightmare under the setting sun, I could barely discern human figures on either side of me. Suddenly, as if by magic, the smoke and dust dissipated. We were left exposed without cover. The entire township had been taken by surprise. People stared at each other, utterly bewildered. In the midst of this chaos, a gunshot rang out, followed by a whistle and a shout of „advance!" We scattered like frightened chickens, each person for themselves. Parents ran, leaving their children behind—such a heartbreaking sight.

With their ruthless attack tactics, the rebels swiftly captured Koidu City and all the mining sites across Kono District. Their speed outmatched the government soldiers, leaving them unable to mount a defense against the relentless RUF. Many neighbors abandoned their homes and sought refuge in the wilderness and other villages.

Due to the escalating intensity of the war, my father decided that we should leave the town, fearing that the rebels might take me if they found us. Following my father's instructions, my stepmother packed a few bundles of clothes and assorted food items. I had to carry some on my head as we navigated through thorny bushes, sharp objects, and crawling animals. Alongside my step-grandma and younger step-brother, as well as our close neighbors, we embarked on a journey to seek refuge in unknown areas.

During this perilous journey, we encountered the horrifying sight of corpses—men, women, and children—scattered throughout the neighborhoods, corners, streets, and roads. The scenes were unforgettable, with vultures feasting on the remains. The memories of that day continue to haunt me.

My father was determined to ensure I remained with him as we progressed. This was because wherever the rebels triumphed, they forcibly recruited children into their ranks. These children were trained to be merciless and even more lethal than their adult counterparts in warfare. A significant reason for this was the administration of hard drugs like cocaine or heroin mixed with marijuana, along with strong distilled rum, to these children.

Young men who were captured were compelled to work in the fields to extract diamonds, which were then traded for weapons and other supplies. Their acts of brutality and massacres aimed to instill widespread fear, and soon enough, the entire town turned into a ghostly enclave.

Leaving behind Koidu City, our treacherous journey led us through hilly terrain, streams, and winding paths until we encountered two elderly women. These women informed us that we were heading for Yormandu. After walking for eight hours, we made a stop at a deserted farmhouse to eat. We repacked our bundles, leaving behind items that proved burdensome on our journey. Five more hours of walking followed, punctuated by stops to find navigable routes. As we sought refuge, most of the villages we came across were deserted.

One school of thought suggested that the villagers had gone to their various farms to hide, while another said that they had abandoned their homes in fear of a possible attack. Along the way, we were often welcomed by dogs with faded and scary growls.

As we journeyed, we asked some villagers how far it was to Yormandu, and they said it was three kilometers away. I hoped they were right. Crossing a grassy path, darkness was descending upon us. Yormandu wasn't far, as supposed, but our feet and bodies told a different story.

The foggy, rough hilly paths near Yormandu will remain in my memory forever. Somewhere in this troubled land, our journey would end, hopefully for only a short period of time. We reached Yormandu after 11 pm, and the night was all about our next move—to sleep. Tired and exhausted, we slept on the back of an abandoned house. What a night it was! Cold winds crept in; our nostrils ensured they had enough, sleep was certain, and we dozed off in the chill with little care for anything but our painful, dusty feet and tender joints. The mental torture was far worse, however, plagued by the things we had seen and the fear of what was to come.

Two days after arriving in Yormandu, the rebels attacked a village called Seidu, which was very close. We had to run for our lives again. Finally, we made it to Kayima, the headquarters town in Sandor Chiefdom, Kono District. This town had become the sanctuary for thousands of Internally Displaced Persons (IDPs) who had fled the invasion forces early in the war. They had become a mass of hungry, dirty, and homeless people living in fear and total despair.

Upon reaching Kayima, we dropped our bundles and backpacks. As a family, we recounted our journey, feeling like weary and exhausted athletes who had crossed the finish line after a long and strenuous marathon, finally breathing a sigh of relief. But only for the time being!

Earlier, as we journeyed, we noticed the lean, hungry, and abandoned children of war congregating near the thatch-roofed houses. We shared portions of our food with them, whatever we had to spare. These kids were orphans, living day by day in makeshift shelters or nearby caves. Some of the older ones were caring for their younger siblings. Amidst the dry heat and humidity, everyone was too preoccupied to think about the welfare and future of these children. It was too painful to even consider.

If I could still recall, when we approached nearby farmhouses, we could see the physical damage caused by the war—destroyed motorbikes and cars along the tracks, deserted villages, and wooden bridges hanging over rivers. We were beginning to realize that our destiny lay directly ahead of us. We saw villages in the thick, dense areas and quickly learned their names, anticipating the questions we might be asked if a rescue party crossed our path. More importantly, in case of an unpleasant encounter with anyone in military attire, be it a soldier or a rebel! We might have pronounced the names of the villages wrongly, but they would be forever associated with the civil war in our minds.

My mind went blank as we crossed a shallow stream. Our group of more than a dozen seized the opportunity to scoop some water using cocoa yam leaves as cups, quenching our parched throats. We were hungry but too frightened to look for food, perhaps cassava tubers or sweet potatoes from old or abandoned farms. One of the young men traveling with us was familiar with the terrain, ensuring he provided navigation and warnings of possible routes leading to dangerous rebel encampments.

We were a group of about 16 that had escaped from Koidu to Yormandu and then to Kayima in the Kono district. Barely a day after our arrival, we noticed a large number of people from different villages. Some were maimed, others had horrifying stories to tell. We were informed that Kayima should not be considered a safe haven. Rumors had it that the rebels had sworn to destroy the town once they took over. Before our arrival, some youths had organized into vigilante groups to secure their town. During one of their raids into the bush, they encountered a young man they suspected of being a spy for the rebels. After handing him over to the soldiers stationed in Kayima, rumors spread that the supposed spy was shot and killed shortly after what seemed like a mock interrogation. This incident reached the ears of the rebels, leading them to vow wrath and vengeance upon Kayima. To worsen matters, Komba Mondeh, a gallant military officer, hailed from that town.

When the threat of an attack by the rebels became evident in Kayima, we decided to move to forest farms located mostly in the dense bushes. After walking for about two hours, our bodies succumbed to the need for food, for survival's sake and to sustain us for the challenging task of trekking through rough and unsuitable paths. Dehydrated from the unforgiving sun and hungry, we stopped for a few hours to prepare something to eat. Our menu was quite limited, as most of us had little or no food. Among our supplies were salt, matchboxes, a few pints of palm oil, and cubes of jumbo maggi. The forest, our new home, was merciless. As we slept on the damp ground, insects relentlessly attempted to crawl into our ears and nostrils, driving us to the brink of insanity.

We gathered some sticks and made a fire to cook whatever we could find in the bushes. This turned out to be a mistake, as the rebels were clever enough to stand at a distance and observe the smoke emanating from the bushes, pinpointing our location. The smoke acted as a tracer, an easy mark to spot. In less than thirty minutes, we heard the rustling of leaves, and we quickly pressed our ears to the ground. The young man who was leading us suddenly stood with a pale look, exclaiming in a hushed tone that ultimately revealed our hiding place. Before we could react, footsteps were approaching or possibly already upon us.

As we bent down to listen and confirm his claim, we were surrounded by shouts of „halt!" Two shots fired into the air brought us to a halt. The rebels had found us. It marked the beginning of a new era, and death seemed inevitable. We were terrified as they appeared, shouting, „You're running away from us? Now that you're caught, you'll have to tell us why you were fleeing!" We tried to appease their anger by saying we understood they were fighting for us and that we weren't running away. They took us, along with the young and older women, back to the Kayima village. Our group consisted of sixteen people.

Women of all ages were raped, abused and molested. Many of the young girls had earlier on tried to costume their looks so as not to appear attractive to the rebels. However smart and thoughtful their ideas were, that did not prevent rebels from their advances as they found pleasure in raping and abusing them till, they agreed to become their 'bush wives'. It was common practice for a beautiful lady to openly declare her admiration for any of the top-ranking rebels so as to evade constant rape and abuse by other rebels. By so doing, any lady would save herself from constant intimidation and harassment from the volatile renegade. She would be accorded with tremendous respect she was mostly addressed as 'the mammy,' meaning the big mama in the camp or simply the Boss' wife.

When drunk or heavily intoxicated with drugs, the rebels took turns to have violent sex with the female victims and sometimes would allow other captured victims to watch as they carried out their beastly acts. Men who were muscular and fit to carry arms were intoxicated (whether they consent or not) and brainwashed them into believing that their cause was genuine. In a country with high illiteracy, they pried on cooked-up revolutionary ideas and the sacrosanct need for a nation-wide emancipation from greedy and corrupt politicians, as they would solemnly infer. Torture was an option for those who resisted before taking a bullet in the head.

Our capture and subsequent abduction became a furor of events and experiences that would impact my life in a giant pincer than I had imagined. As a young lad of eleven, my lean and timid appearance eliminated the possibility to lift the most available weapon by then, the AK47 assault rifle. However, I was deemed a prime candidate to become a child soldier and a load carrier. We were frog marched into an encampment that was rooted into the deep forest – a jungle, so to speak. It was my first experience to be so far away from home. We were sorted into three groups, each led by a certain commander.

My step mother, together with her son and ailing mother were in another group. We walked our hands placed above our heads through the forest, over rusty leaves which suggested that the path was unused before. It was a long queue with young lads in front, women and girls in the middle and the aged and young adults behind. Each group had at least fifteen rebels, all armed and forming a half circle around their captives.

We parted ways with my father at Yormandu before any unfortunate events could occur. This decision was made because he chose to stay behind and oversee the house along with other remaining properties.

We made no noise as we walked with each praying for his/her life to be spared. We walked for about half an hour until we were told to stop. It was at this juncture that we split parties and all three groups headed for different routes. The leading commanders made fist bumps and signs as if to note they will meet later at a known spot. Our group continued to walk an extra 20 minutes until we arrived at a spot which was hidden behind a cleft-like ridge. We descended the small route that was covered with leaves and shrubs, a ghastly feeling gripped my body and mind and the repugnant smell of dead bodies only confirmed my premonition. This positioned my body to be alert and fit for whatever ordeal that lay await to welcome us to our new abode. And yes indeed, we were!

The scenes and images I experienced remain vivid – looting, rape, inhumane behavior and sheer savagery was commonplace. As we passed by, each of the men looked fiercely at us; one can smell the aura of decay that emitted from their unkempt bodies. By every assessment, it would be fair to assume that water and bathing in general was a luxury that was reserved only for the "Wannabe Commando Leaders." This camp was unlike any other settlement that I had seen in my teen life. The entire protocol and affairs were strictly bizarre and the rebels took every sort of rank in the military that suit their ambition.

Respect and the right to give orders were only won through gallantry and total display of wickedness. As such, every one wielding a gun sought means to make a show of themselves through acts of wickedness and inhumane conducts – boasting and public bragging was akin to displaying one's resume as if vetting for a befitting job. During the day, we were taught to shoot a gun. I was drugged with a combination of petrol gas and gun powder called 'bom-bom'. This routine was followed by the normal long speeches of intimidation and brain-washing – a task which they mastered and delivered clearly.

Their objective was to manipulate our minds, making us believe they held the exclusive role of saviors for the country. What ultimately safeguarded me, as well as fellow like-minded thinkers who resisted their allure, were the haunting memories of the brutal massacre I personally witnessed during their initial assault. The images of devastation and their callous disregard for the numerous lives they claimed to be redeeming remained ingrained within me.

Beyond engaging in warfare, the ordinary recruits undergo a plethora of experiences that can at times prove more indelible and traumatic than the battles themselves. Reflecting on the past, it marked the commencement of a monumental journey that would forever remain etched in memory. Like many recruits, I was completely oblivious to the trials that lay ahead and the destinations that future assignments would lead me to. The primary trial that every novice recruit encounters is the rigorous process of basic and advanced training, particularly within the infantry. Completing these demanding two weeks of training and enduring the challenges posed leads to a significant acclimatization to military life.

After several days of practice, I was now able to do up to thirty push-ups in a go. Completing this feat, one was considered fit to carry firearms and I was now to be trained the following week in handling weapons which I presumed will be solely centered on how to kill people indiscriminately, and was also forced to inhale the stench of alcohol and marijuana, thereby, making dreadful in an encounter with opposition- had to be one of the worst experiences.

Both my stepmother and her son found themselves in different groups at separate locations, likely undergoing experiences similar to the challenges I was confronting. As I endeavored to endure these unclassified actions, an immense emotional burden weighed upon me, making the military drills appear even more formidable.

Our camp adhered to a strict schedule of events and training sessions. In the light of day, the rebels instructed us in the ways of child soldiers, while under the cover of night, they engaged in acts of destruction and looting. Whenever they targeted a home, the rebels ransacked each dwelling, seizing everything from food supplies to valuable items that could be easily carried.

We were transformed into small units of trainee soldiers and designated as the ‚carriers'. Our responsibility was to transport the plundered belongings to our remote camp nestled deep within the dense forest. It was there that Abdul, another young man, became my sole connection to a „forced family." He happened to be the son of my stepmother's cousin and was roughly my age. Together, we provided each other with a semblance of sanity amidst the chaos. I first encountered him at 10 Turner Street in Koidu Town, before the war, when he came to visit his aunt, my stepmother. He was my lone companion, yet sadly, I have not laid eyes on him since the war's conclusion, nor do I possess any knowledge of his whereabouts.

The individual overseeing my unit was known as Rambo. He exhibited extreme brutality, taking pleasure in subjecting others to torture and mutilation. He resorted to particularly disturbing methods, such as inserting sharpened sticks into the sensitive areas of women who declined his advances. Throughout the day, Rambo subjected us to relentless drills and harsh treatment. Among his preferred methods of torment, if we made even a minor mistake or failed to meet his standards, he would bind our arms and secure our elbows together behind our backs, pushing them to an unnatural and painful position. This contortion was almost impossible to achieve, resulting in the elbows never quite touching while forcing the chest bone at the center of the torso to rupture through the skin upon contact, causing severe injury. Although this didn't always lead to fatalities, many individuals succumbed to untreated wounds caused by the protrusion of the chest bone through their skin.

Living under the ever-present specter of Rambo's fury, we were no strangers to his adamant declaration that those who dared oppose the quest for our nation's liberation were nothing short of traitors, deserving of the harshest retribution. His speech, punctuated by a stammer, was a vessel for his unyielding callousness, as he contended that mercy equated to vulnerability. In his eyes, only those with hearts as immense as his own were qualified to guide a nation, a belief he ardently championed. His delight in acts of violence and cruelty was unsettling, his boasts about his ruthless exploits matched only by his eagerness to elevate individuals who shared his merciless ideology.

Our existence was marked by a relentless fear, a constant companion as we endured both physical torment and psychological anguish. Under Rambo's leadership, we faced the ordeal of famine, with infested rations as our sustenance. His twisted logic argued that abundant food would be a breeding ground for lethargy.

Enduring nearly four harrowing months in the clutches of the rebels, the ECOMOG forces finally took action, launching air strikes that targeted our encampment. These strikes were executed by military fighter jets, referred to as ‚alpha jets,' dispatched by the ECOWAS military observer group to bolster the Sierra Leone government. Initially, the distant sounds were brushed aside as insignificant, a result of our concealed location and the sheltering forest around us, lulling us into a false sense of security. But that illusion shattered when the jets unleashed their fury, bombarding us from above. Pandemonium erupted, compelling everyone, rebels included, to flee the relentless assault. Amidst the chaos, the rebels sought to retaliate against the airborne threat, inadvertently creating an opening for us, their captives, to escape in the midst of the turmoil.

Our pursuit of freedom took a treacherous turn, exposing us to the scorching sun, eerie wilderness sounds, and wounds inflicted by thorns and blades. Stranded in an unforgiving wilderness, we found kinship with others who had fled different attacks, swiftly coalescing into a group of over 200 displaced souls—mostly women, children, and young men. The looming specter of death became an uninvited companion, a shadow that never left our side. Remarkably, post-attack, it became evident that the rebels and the captives had fled in opposite directions. Despite our dispersal during the assault, a natural inclination pulled us back together into small units, ultimately culminating in a band of former captives. The wilderness became our sole sanctuary as we traversed ghost towns ravaged by rebel onslaughts, journeying tirelessly for hours on end.

We pressed on until we found ourselves three miles away from the Guinean border. Despite our attempts to rest, thoughts of our harrowing encounter with the rebels prevented us from finding any solace. Eventually, we arrived in a town named Faranah, only to be met with disappointment. As refugees, we were dismayed to discover that entering Guinea required funds we didn't possess.

The Guineans were well aware of the influx of Sierra Leoneans into their country, thus imposing a specific fee known as the ‚entry tax'. Unfortunately, none of our group had the necessary money. This situation forced us to establish a camp near the border, in constant fear of potential pursuit by the rebels.

Communication with my mother in Freetown was an insurmountable challenge. With no mobile phones and the landlines dead since before the war, I couldn't reach her. My maternal instinct strongly conveyed her longing to hear from me, a sentiment any mother would feel when her child is trapped behind enemy lines.

The three months we spent seeking asylum at the Guinea border were marked by unimaginable hardships. Our camp was makeshift, and sustenance was derived from whatever we could salvage from nature. Bonded by the horrors of violence and war, we became a makeshift family, our conversations limited due to the shared trauma we all witnessed.

At the border, our camp was filled with inconsolable grief, teeth gnashing, and anguished cries. In their minds, the brutal atrocities of their loved ones played out vividly—killings, torture, abductions, rape, and amputations—while they were helpless to intervene, left with no choice but to flee for their lives.

My own experience on the battlefield was nightmarish, yet paradoxically, I never once fired a bullet. This seemingly perplexing fact was a result of my lack of enthusiasm for such acts. My unit's commander never detected any willingness in my eyes to engage in combat, an unintentional blessing. Instead, I was relegated to carrying plundered goods alongside other boys and victims. I endured a grueling two years behind enemy lines (1992–1994).

My family and I were captured three consecutive times within those two years. This also occurred at a specific point in time when I was completely separated from the rest of my family. My final escape in 1994 came about when the „Alpha Jets" of the ECOMOG were patrolling the airspace of the rebel zone where I was. Alongside other captives, we seized the opportunity and had to run for our lives. By the Grace of God, I managed to escape on a clean slate!

Following my „lucky escape" from the rebels, I had to journey on foot to Masshingbi in the Tonkolili District, located north of Sierra Leone. There, I also reunited with my step-mother. I was a complete stranger in Masshingbi. It also happened that my mother's friend, Fatu Tejan, went to buy goods in Masshingbi, and that's where we met.

Upon her return to Freetown, she informed my mum about me. By then, I could tell that my mother had lost hope of ever seeing me alive again in one piece. This was because, as she later told me, she had searched all the available amputee camps in the capital and even checked the Connaught Government Hospital Morgue in the hopes of finding my remains by chance.

Finally, I managed to make it back to Freetown and into the warm and loving embrace of my „sweet mother." Tears of joy rolled down our eyes as we embraced each other.

Chapter 4

Education for Transformation

As with any child, education is a must! Immediately after reconciling with my loving mother, I had to go to school. However, due to the constraints my mother was facing—perhaps a typical reason was the impact of the war when her business wasn't flourishing, along with the mixed feelings she had nurtured since my abduction—meeting my schooling needs was challenging for her. This prompted her to send me away. I had to relocate to my paternal uncle, his wife, and their children to continue schooling.

When I shed light on my primary education, my enrollment in Class 5 at Saint Edward's Primary School marked the beginning of my educational transformation after the bitter experience with the rebels. I took the National Primary School Examination (NPSE) in 1996 and gained admission to Prince of Wales School, my chosen institution.

I went to Prince of Wales with strong determination to succeed. However, as time went on and the conflict escalated, with Freetown coming under attack, we lost a year of schooling. The government introduced an expedited learning program called the remedial term. I took the Basic Education Certificate Examination (BECE) in 2000, which is the Junior Secondary School (JSS) National Examination required for admission to Senior Secondary School. In 2003, I sat for the West Africa Senior Secondary School Certificate Examination (WASSCE), a crucial exam that marked the completion of my High School education at Prince of Wales School. WASSCE is a prerequisite for university entry, requiring a minimum pass in five subjects.

If I were to take you back to the tense periods of the brutal war, specifically on May 25, 1997, there was a coup d'état masterminded by Johnny Paul Koroma, followed by a rebel invasion in Freetown. This led to the overthrow of the democratically elected Sierra Leone Peoples' Party-SLPP led government of Alhaji Dr. Ahmad Tejan Kabbah by soldiers turned rebels. ECOMOG forces eventually stormed Freetown to end the nine-month siege by these rebels, commonly known as ‚Sobels.'

History will always remember Johnny Paul Koroma and his group for committing gruesome acts across the country as they retreated from ECOMOG-controlled areas. These Sobels, during their retreat, vowed to carry out what they termed "Operation No Living Thing." This was manifested through rapes, killings, destruction of public and private structures, looting, abductions, and other atrocities as they traversed the dense peninsular villages.

During this frightful period, schooling came to a complete halt across the country. I suffered from severe post-traumatic stress disorder (PTSD), which manifested as frequent nightmares and bouts of depression. Dealing with such psychological issues as a minor left me feeling sad, as the actions of these rebel soldiers reminded me of my experiences as a child soldier.

After the military intervention subsided and the rebels were pushed out of the capital, life slowly returned amidst the grief of those who had lost their lives and properties. With nothing to ease the accumulated devastation, the concept of collateral damage sufficed to describe the scars left behind by the war. Schools were promoted en masse across the country to make up for the lost academic year. I was promoted to JSS 2 in 1998.

Although I was staying with my paternal relatives, my mother didn't shift all my responsibilities to them. She often sent allowances for lunch and transportation to support my education at Prince of Wales School. She entrusted these funds to Aunty Edna and Mama Stevens, who were in-laws to my niece and were kind neighbors. Despite facing constraints, my mother never succumbed to obstacles. She continued this support even when I relocated to a family friend's house after my BECE in Wellington. I had to endure similar domestic chores in this new household, but as always, I maintained the spirit of my mother—holding my head high and focusing on the ultimate goal: ‚Education for Transformation.'

In 2003, just before I took the final exams in secondary school, my mother made it clear that she couldn't afford my university expenses. However, as a determined young man, I took the bold step of obtaining a University Application Form at one of Sierra Leone's finest universities, Fourah Bay College-FBC. I chose to study Peace and Conflict Studies, a discipline introduced after the war and enshrined in the Faculty of Social Science and Law.

With the initiative to pursue a university education and my mother's clear message that she couldn't fund my tertiary education, I immediately got in touch with my niece, Christiana Zainab Stevens, who was the daughter of my cousin (my father's niece) and was about to migrate to the United States. Theresa, my niece, had already relocated to the USA. Zainab, as she was commonly called, agreed to help with my university fees, but with a condition attached: I had to achieve good grades in the WASSCE. When the results were released, I had achieved good grades, and Zainab fulfilled her promise. This support provided the foundation for my success today. The assistance from Zainab and her immediate family circle was the sole reason for my achievements, serving as the key that unlocked the doors to both my professional life and academic progress.

I can also tell you that my university education, with specific reference to my course of study (Peace and Conflict Studies), was the pinnacle of my life's transformation. It was a remarkable experience, and I had the privilege of encountering wonderful individuals like Mr. Desmond George Williams and Dr. Memunatu Pratt, who provided significant support throughout my studies.

Chapter 5

Standing Tall to Life's Challenges

Though university education was the climax to my empowerment and transformation, I always had it in mind, that I was destined for greater things ahead of me. Trust me; pursuing university education is no child's play and especially when you are living on hopes and dreams. There is always this status quo of accepting the university life. What I meant by this? You have to prepare your mind, body and soul.

FBC, as the university is popularly called, is situated at the peak of a place known as Mount Aureol in present day Freetown. Going for lectures every day, is like per taken on a marathon. I had to walk up and down the university and rarely take a cab for and after lectures. My poor and humble background obviously made this possible. If you happened to visit FBC or gained admission at this university, there is always this popular slogan amongst students who could not afford to take a cab- 'sam u dae canal?' Which literally mean in Krio: asking your buddy if he is walking his way home after lectures or going for lectures? Basically, this question is asked to show commitment to the "canal route" which I always have fond memories of. This popular route will empty to other roads that cut between Kissy Road, one of the leading roads into the country's central business district of Freetown, where I always find my way to Wellington at my maternal grandpa's resident.

Sealing the Diploma Programme of the Peace and Conflict Studies course I opted for, I had to do an Internship Programme which went out successfully at the Network Movement for Justice and Development

(NMJD), a local advocacy organization. During my internship at NMJD, I showed so much commitment that I won the admiration of Morlai Kamara who was the Programme Manager for Economic Justice at NMJD Kenema Regional Office, and who agreed to take care of my welfare after I was posted to Kenema, and my only responsibility was to work with the other interns in the provincial areas. Though NMJD was not giving stipends to interns, but luckily, my batch of interns were fortunate to be given stipends on a monthly basis, but only if we work in the provinces. I considered such an offer as a huge boost in transforming my life financially and professionally. On that note, I had to encourage my fellow intern – Nancy Koroma to accept the offer which would broaden our academic and social horizons.

After Nancy accepted to join this exploration, we left Freetown for our various stations. She left for Bo City while I head for Kenema City, which cities are in the south and eastern region of the country respectively.

If I could use words to describe my commitment to NMJD, I was like an "errand boy" who members of staff could count on to undertake any activity swiftly and diligently. I was always on my heels to deliver messages or carryout the next job. Because of my commitment to my areas of responsibilities, Morlai Kamara offered me his bed room in Kenema, which actually saved me the worries of accommodation in the Kenema Township. I was mentored on Programming and Activism, and there was one key personality, I considered as a role model in addition to Morlai Kamara, Karim Bah who was the Programs Manager for the NMJD-Youth Empowerment for the Mano River Basin, who also happened to be my supervisor during my internship.

Working for NMJD exposed me to some quite exciting learning curves on office setup and implementations of project. My first real test in project implementation was when I played a major part on a project to be executed in Bo City. Karim Bah exposed to some kind of responsibility that I was never opportune to, he challenged me to manage the sum of Le twenty-five million which by then was a little over eight thousand three hundred United States Dollars which was meant to entire program youth engagement on the Poverty Reduction Paper in Bo. Honestly, it was a responsibility that nearly drove me crazy. This was because I had to repeatedly verify on a daily basis what is left of the money and to also ensure that I collate all receipts of the necessary expenditures. The experience of managing such money was like hell. I had sleepless nights praying that all went well and every single penny under my possession is accounted for thoroughly. I could confess to you that such project undertaken in Bo was a huge National Youth Conference, and there I also had the opportunity to meet with many advocates across the country and I learnt so many things from them and the youths that participated.

In my quiet and personal times, I paced about with ideas that would be needed to factor youth voices into nation building and attaining sustainable developmental standards on a country-wide spectrum. I was to later learn the acronym HIPC which stands for Heavily Indebted Poor Countries of which Sierra Leone was clearly not an exception.

It was only then that I began to realize that life had so much to offer and nature herself cannot be the only giver. It became further clear that all we need to make the world better is to give a little more; if we give in a little of our time; a little of our energies; a little of our space; a little of our belief; a little of our effort; all will boil down to making the world a better place.

My work with NMJD continued to avail me with opportunities and more moments that will involve my entire body, mind and spirit. I also learnt a lot as I engaged in the Campaign for Just Mining, one of the projects under NMJD which begets its concept from the Economic Justice Program – an umbrella project that seeks to ensure fair deals within the mining sector. I became a small but zealous voice that campaigned against unfair treatment to miners and land owners in mining areas especially in Kono. Equally with the same zest was my supervisor on this project, the late Esther Kamara who was fearless and always ready to pry into unjust matters. We conducted interviews and close encounters with victims of mining and hazardous disasters.

In my expedition of such a fine project of Campaign for Just Mining, I had the opportunity once more to return to in history I will never forget, a place where I was abducted as a boy and forcefully enlisted into a fighting force as a child soldier: Kono.

Kono being the hub for diamond mining across the country, has so many complaints from victims in the mining sites who expressed their disgust over the blatant disregard and disrespect of their lives by the thunderous dynamite blasts carried out by the then Koidu Holdings Limited in Koidu which was a renowned mining institution. Together with journalists and other advocacy groups, routine interviews with victims of structural damages to their houses by the fragments of the kimberlitic blast were conducted.

Apparently, with our video interviews with victims and snapshots of sites, we realized that indeed homes and properties of the locals were destroyed by such gruesome practice. We were so keen in unearthing the truth that it got to a point that my supervisor, Esther

Kamara of blessed memory and I were arrested and taken to the Tankoro Police Station for questioning; only for us to become subjects to intimidation and wanton harassment acting on orders from mining companies and government officials.

Our wallets, video camera, recorder and phones were confiscated. Luckily for me, I was very swift to have removed the memory chip from the camera slot and hid it quickly out of sight and reach by the police officers. After spending some rough hours in police custody, we were released – our phones were turned inside out, our recorder searched but unfortunately, little did they know that the chip was way hidden inside my shoe. At the end they had no tangible evidence to lay their claim. Abu Brima, the Executive Director of NMJD sought our release. This ugly incident with the police, clearly

Chapter 6

Turning Scars into Stars

As a child, there is always the desire to achieve greatness in life with fancy dreams and aspirations. Moving forward in life, many of the dreams and aspirations we heard during childhood are likely to change as destiny takes a new course during the transition from adolescence to adulthood. It is inevitable that some dreams may come true while others may not. Fate consistently influences human lives. However, a specific and effective way to succeed in life is by believing in yourself where others have let you down. Believing in yourself and maintaining a positive mental attitude put you in control of your life, enabling you to set goals that bring you closer to your dreams.

It is common for us to daydream about our ambitions when pretending to be lawyers, doctors, engineers, bankers, police officers, pilots, soldiers, and more. These scenarios are often distinct from the dreams we have while asleep.

As I immersed myself in various human rights and advocacy issues, I began to comprehend the intricate details that constitute social work. I started daydreaming about my future and grappling with unanswered questions: What do I need to learn? What career path do I want to pursue? What obstacles stand in the way of my career goals? How will I envision myself in 5 to 10 years? How can I contribute to making the world a better place? These questions allowed me to realize that the key to achieving my dreams lies in taking action. This realization prompted me to establish specific goals and guiding principles for my life, shaping my world.

Working within Non-Governmental Organizations and Civil Society presents both advantages and challenges. The public may mistakenly perceive a non-governmental officer's role as straightforward, involving a high salary and fringe benefits, which is far from accurate. Sometimes, the sacrifices outweigh the benefits. In certain institutions, the expectation of extra compensation for extra hours worked doesn't align with reality, as an organization's vision often surpasses the idea of having just a job and emphasizes having a career. While you may have your plans and strategies, their execution might have direct and indirect impacts on those around you.

For instance, your aspirations might revolve around ideals like world peace, providing food for the less privileged, addressing homelessness, aiding victims of rape and domestic violence, or assisting victims of natural disasters. These ideals for humanitarianism have been my lifelong pursuits, especially considering my experience as a child soldier. I made a solemn pact with my conscience that if I believe in an ideal, I must also believe in myself and my ability to manifest those ideals.

With these thoughts in mind, I started acting in ways that reinforced my commitment to humanitarian causes. Recognizing that most plans need to be set in motion long before they become goals, I became increasingly focused on my humanitarian endeavors, avoiding distractions that would offer immediate but fleeting gratification. This approach became my life's guiding principle, enabling me to progress step by step toward my ambitions.

Our life journeys extend beyond physical limitations, fears, strengths, and weaknesses that define our paths – aspects often beyond our control at the outset. Opportunities, much like people, come in diverse forms and sizes, appearing at various points along our individual destinies. We all aspire to reach the culmination of our success stories.

However, the realization of our triumphs only arrives when we consciously choose to overcome challenges with determination and resilience, ultimately redeeming ourselves. As my redemption days approached, I recognized that this transformation wasn't a one-time occurrence. I acknowledged that I was seizing an opportunity to reshape my life, reconcile with my past, and discover my true self.

Before contemplating the future and our desired identities, we must first understand our authentic selves. This awareness unveils insights into our aspirations as we age. Such self-discovery provides illumination regarding our needs, motives, and emotions, thereby paving a path to explore our inner landscape. Recognizing my true emotions was instrumental in uncovering both positive and negative qualities and skills, which could either propel me towards my goals or hinder my progress.

Interacting with various individuals taught me a few essential lessons. Avoiding the pretense of pleasing others is crucial. Such behavior can hinder your ability to set personal standards that positively influence you and your surroundings. If actions are driven solely by the aim to please others, you must accept the outcomes, which often don't align with your desires. At this juncture, I realized the symbiotic relationship between responsibility and leadership.

Interestingly, attempting to conform or imitate others can breed self-doubt, making it challenging to believe in oneself and pursue goals wholeheartedly. Overcoming self-doubt and ensuring future success necessitated doing what I believed to be right, even during my internships.

While managing various facets of my youthful life, I found it essential to engrain the ABCs of life into my mindset. I adopted the practice of consistently reminding myself that I aimed for personal growth and the development of self-esteem. These guiding principles served as my blueprints. My journey began with introspection to ascertain if my ambitious goals conflicted with other personal aspirations.

Subsequently, I contemplated the amount of time required to align these goals with the available support systems. This led to a multitude of questions, each answered by dedicating effort to specific tasks. Continuously reassessing my dedication enabled me to identify my opportunity costs.

In order to achieve success in one endeavour, it may sometimes be necessary to relinquish something else. As daring as this may sound, it demands making close-call choices that often require significant courage. In Economics, this concept is referred to as 'Opportunity Cost.' One notable challenge arose when I had to decide between gaining more field-related experience and opting for lucrative means to meet my personal needs. Despite the financial necessity, I risked missing out on valuable experience from my daily field operations. This hidden cost needed careful consideration to align with my goals, and the sincerest price I had to pay was my earnest dedication to prioritize my job above all else, regardless of the cost.

Another crucial aspect of my life is self-discipline, with overcoming procrastination being paramount. I coined a mantra that consistently reminded me to eliminate wasted time. Thus, I learned to structure daily routines by establishing priorities to guide my time management. Working in the field, especially in areas lacking internet services, could impose undue pressure on a social worker. Often, weariness might lead to deferring tasks, which, over time, can result in feeling overwhelmed and either quitting or not attempting at all. I frequently experienced this, yet my commitment to my principles made me feel guilty and intensely pressured about unfinished work. Nonetheless, with a determined mindset, I held onto this guilt until I rectified matters. The satisfaction and relief from doing the right thing were unparalleled.

Hence, a motivating lesson I gleaned from colleagues concerned identifying and pursuing five essential aspects: relationships, education, career, personal development, and leisure. These components, as they enlightened me, constitute a well-rounded life. Although this might not have made immediate sense, I later discovered that they formed the core focus of any pursuit or vocation. Self-discipline proved instrumental in guiding me to make informed life decisions, curbing youthful excesses, even when it required giving up personal desires.

At one point, I evaluated myself, reflecting on the most impactful aspects of my personal growth. The recurring answer was solemn and poignant. The fear of failure consistently drove me to strive for greatness, if not success. Failing tasks during my youth triggered emotional turmoil, instilling in me a deep sense of breakdown. They say bravery is distinct from recklessness, involving control over fear when it matters. This idea resonated with me as I made sacrifices, relinquishing precious elements of my life like family, friends, and cultural ties for broader social ethics and expectations. However, it shaped me into a resilient character as I ascended the ladder of service, propelled by the belief that I have a purpose in serving humanity.

Another crucial goal for my career development was embracing risks. This required shedding certain fears or beliefs that might have previously held me back. I grasped that taking risks necessitates trust and often relies on the judgment of others, accepting feedback while anticipating potential unpleasant surprises. Embracing these changes opened new opportunities to interact with colleagues and express either appreciation or concerns about their work or behavior. This propelled my interpersonal skills faster than expected, affirming my belief that risk-taking outweighs the risk of failure. By shifting negative thoughts to positive ones, we transform the improbable into possible and turn nays into yeas. It's a leap worth taking.

Reflecting on the choices I made throughout my educational journey, I often ask myself: ‚Do I regret sacrificing the comfort of home and hanging out with friends?' The answer has consistently been a resounding no. In hindsight, I don't entertain regrets or dwell on sacrifices. Instead, they give me purpose to chase my dreams and live an extraordinary life with a distinctive narrative. Guided by these principles, my life has steered towards my passion and dream of being a humanitarian and advocate, standing up for disaster victims and the less privileged. This purpose grants me a sense of belonging that helps me appreciate challenging days and manage my anxieties.

Despite encountering uncomfortable situations in my youth, my primary challenge was not seeking public recognition, but embracing a sense of responsibility, accepting life's blows, and contributing positively as we strive for sustenance. My wish is for my story to inspire fulfillment, helping others rise against challenges and adversity. Devastating circumstances can act as springboards, and regardless of how unusual our circumstances might be, we have the power to transform our scars into shining stars.

Each of us possesses a unique story – one of despair and courage, loss and victory, past and present. By harnessing our stories, we can find solutions to ongoing social issues that threaten our happiness. I am using my narrative to infuse hope into the hopeless, reminding

everyone that light always awaits at the tunnel'

Chapter 7

At the Behest of a Call

Completing my course at Fourah Bay College left me with mixed feelings about the options I might have to consider to make my life a successful one. Doing an internship with the Network Movement for Justice and Development (NMJD) presented many opportunities that broadened my mindset about social work and building a career out of it.

By the end of my tenure with NMJD, I had written an article that went viral in one of the leading internet magazines called "Mines and Communities." My shared opinion was met with both acclaim and criticism, but the acclaim far outweighed the criticism. This boosted my stance and confidence in proactive advocacy. When mentors like Morlai Kamara, Charles Lahai, and Ngolo Katta applauded my passion in this direction, it was clear that I shouldn't give in to any distractions. The article I had written, titled 'What NMJD Has Taught Me,' expressed my expectations, experiences, and challenges in my line of duty. This title later became a moniker by which I became known. My mentors would call me this name whenever I interacted with them, as this caption echoed the various encounters that social work would bring to my journey.

As I read related articles dealing with humanitarian interventions, I became familiar with the concept of the right to humanitarian intervention. This concept arose primarily due to the shame felt by the international community over its failure to take action during the massacre of the Tutsis by the Hutus in Rwanda. The right of intervention was invoked during the Kosovo War when Serbs used terror to expel the ethnic majority from their homeland. This concept was later renamed and widely became known as "the Responsibility to Protect." It was agreed that „each individual State has the responsibility to protect its populations from genocide, war crimes, ethnic cleansing, and crimes against humanity."

The provisions of the United Nations Charter drew my attention, and a sense of responsibility dawned on me due to the shame I felt for my motherland, combined with the shock from my past as a former child soldier. I felt a strong need to take proactive stances, similar to how the international community, through the United Nations, assumes responsibility to address humanitarian appeals when a state fails to do so.

Perhaps making such an appeal would require a miracle, but one thing was certain: my drive to become a voice for others was deeply rooted, fueled by substantial reasons to strive for change. Speaking of miracles, I had saved this aspect for a more opportune time like this, to narrate three major occurrences in my life that were nothing short of miraculous. It was definitely worth the wait to share these personal miracles in this chapter. Let me take this opportunity to share one miraculous story.

Back in Kono, during my second capture by the RUF, I was among other civilians and prisoners of war. The RUF wanted to send a strong message, and we were to become couriers of a message imprinted on us as a lasting identity. We were lined up, waiting to be called one by one, with a choice between a "short sleeve or a long sleeve." The meaning behind this was to cut off your arm, either at the wrist for „short sleeve" or just below the wrist for „long sleeve." There were thirteen of us, and we prayed fervently for divine intervention. I realized I was the eighth in line. Victims before me had their hands chopped off, and the scene was gruesome.

Three young men and two middle-aged women were amputated right in front of me. They were accused of collaborating with the ECOMOG forces. As they cried in pain, I saw them smearing the stumps of their amputated limbs in the soil to stop the bleeding, while some used cocoa leaves to serve as a natural bandage.

Two individuals were ahead of me, and one of them happened to be my close friend, Abdul. I couldn't bear to watch as they severed his hand, but the sound of the machete and his agonizing screams are etched into my memory forever. After this horrific ordeal, it was almost my turn – another child soldier in line. However, it was at this moment, seemingly providential, that the ECOMOG Military Jet Fighter Aircraft emerged in the sky, accompanied by a deafening roar. Chaos erupted instantly at the rebel checkpoint; even the rebels themselves scattered in all directions. Shots were fired, and the jet fighter executed a swift U-turn, heading toward the source of the gunfire. It retaliated swiftly, shrouding the surroundings in smoke and dust. Everyone sought cover, and we fled in various directions, propelled solely by the instinct to survive, without caring about our path to safety or potential capture.

After running for nearly thirty minutes, the dense bush provided sanctuary once more, marking my first miraculous escape. Given different circumstances, my story could have taken a drastically different turn.

Aware that capture equated to certain death, we traversed both day and night for five consecutive days, forsaking rest and sustenance. Finally, we reached a town under the occupation of the Civil Defense Force, known colloquially as the Kamajors – a militia group. These individuals essentially operated as vigilantes, backed by the government to thwart rebel assaults. Despite their lack of comprehensive military knowledge, they struggled to implement screening procedures that could discern between rebels and non-rebels. Consequently, they herded us into an exposed area and detained us as suspected rebels. The relentless sun showed us no mercy as we endured endless days, yearning for someone to come and vouch for our innocence, convincing the guards of our non-rebel status. This situation was akin to leaping out of the frying pan and into the fire.

Once again, we found ourselves captive, labeled as spies and collaborators. The narrative maintained that collaborators exacerbated the war, resulting in both factions dealing with them ruthlessly and without mercy.

I began losing all sense of hope as I found myself so far away from home. In my despair, little did I know that my second miracle was about to unfold. On a fateful day, after spending two days in captivity, a woman I had never seen before, and would never see again, arrived at the militia camp. She gazed at me in the guarded pen cell and took her time walking by, staring at me slowly but repeatedly. She was unfamiliar to me, and I to her. Even in my hopeless state, I managed to smile at her, recognizing her as a motherly figure like mine. She left our guarded area, and I wondered if I would ever see her again. Not long after her departure from the civil defense camp, one of the captains approached me and informed me that a woman had identified me, leading to my release.

This was unbelievable. At first, I stood speechless, gazing in wonder at who this woman might be and why she had pleaded for my freedom. As the Bible scripture, Psalm 91:11–12, says: 'For he will give His angels charge concerning you, to guard you in your ways. They will bear you up in their hands, that you do not strike your foot against a stone'. I've always believed that there are angels in disguise, no matter how dire our circumstances may appear. My release is proof of that. I searched for this woman who had made my freedom possible, but she was nowhere to be found. Since that day, I've never laid eyes on her again. I was now free but had nowhere to go, still in my teens. I was like a wandering soul, having lived in the bush for so long. All I had were the ragged clothes on my back and my friend Abdul for company, ensuring his amputated hand remained infection-free.

Eventually, we arrived in the town of Magburaka, and I became a homeless street child. I would sleep on people's porches, abandoned benches, under market tables, or in mini shops—anywhere my worn-out body could find comfort. I begged for food and washed dishes in local cookery shops in exchange for meals. My stepmother later found me, in a dire state herself. Financially destitute, she sent me to sell all her personal belongings, such as necklaces, rings, watches, and clothing, just to buy food for us.

I was only fifteen years old, yet I had experienced unspeakable horrors. From 1997 to 1998, I had lived the life of a child soldier, a runaway in the bush, a purposeless vagabond, and yet, a child of miracles. Painful memories and haunting images from what I had witnessed were numerous, but my mother refused to let my future be defined by my past. I am forever grateful to her for the sacrifices she made to send me back to school. One of her jobs was breaking up rocks for sale. With the help of burning tires placed atop the rocks, she usually hired strongmen to crack them first, then she would break them into smaller pieces for sale in the construction trade.

Sometimes we hastily draw conclusions and succumb to despair, even when our despair could align with our callings. Therefore, it would be unwise to infer that individuals with shattered lives or backgrounds cannot make a difference. One of the promises of human faith, as stated in the Holy Bible, is that there is always hope, even in the most challenging situations.

Reintegrating into society after all I had been through was not easy. Fortunately, my background was not widely known, so I could attend school without facing stigma. It was a slow process, but I managed to reintegrate into society. Eventually, I began sharing my story in more open forums, encouraged by a priest who became a father figure to me: Monsignor Dan Sullivan, whose memory is blessed. He played such a pivotal role that I named my daughter after him, Daniella. I met him in 2011 when I started working at Caritas Freetown. He is the driving force behind my autobiography.

Chapter 8

Being Human in Humanity

My first job as a campaigner in the nonprofit world and humanitarian program under the Economic Justice Program at NMJD was met with sincere devotion to become a voice for the voiceless. This led me to work closely on critical issues with other renowned institutions like the Center for the Coordination of Youth Activities (CCYA) and the Women's Refugee Commission (WRC) as a Youth Advisory member for the out-of-school youth initiative program—an advocacy institution based in New York, United States of America.

I played active roles in voicing various concerns faced by youths across the country. These concerns ranged from economic and social injustice to sexual violence, rape, unfair treatment by law enforcers, discrimination, deprivation, drug abuse, child trafficking, child labor, domestic violence, and family-related problems. The list goes on and on. I also had the opportunity to serve as a board member for the acclaimed organization ENCISS, where I was entrusted as a youth advocate on issues of national interest between young people and state actors.

As someone who is a staunch devotee to the ideals of social justice and activism, among others, influenced most of the things I did that contributed in one way or another to national development. There was a particular period in 2006 when, together with other institutions, I played an active role in advocating for the government to review the National Youth Policy, which at the time was outdated. I made poignant contributions through various quotations, articles, and broadcasts in Freetown and the world at large, which was done in consonance with other organizations to ensure a facelift to the National Youth Policy. Though challenging, the efforts went well in the House of Parliament.

The previous youth policy was set up in 2003 after the war, but it soon ran its course as it poorly reflected the many new realities experienced by post-war Sierra Leone. Some of these realities were quite visible in the daily engagements of the many youths who were affected, either directly or indirectly, by the war and were going through some sort of post-traumatic stress disorder, PTSD. This heralded a period when violent and riotous conduct by young people became the order of the day. The nation itself was in much need of healing and total repair. Growing up in a population with high levels of illiteracy, I experienced firsthand how youths were becoming targets for manipulation by politicians.

Through my participation in various activities targeting youths, I was able to become a strong vocal source that empathically pitched the concerns of youths. I became one of the active voices that spoke against the perpetration of youth-led actions that would result in violence and further create instability in our war-torn nation. Despite deploying efforts using various mediums like radio and television broadcasts, all aimed at reforming and stabilizing the mindset of future leaders.

My activism was primarily focused on engaging young people in constructive dialogues through conducting programs that would add value and true meaning to their sense of identity as citizens of my Sierra Leone. As part of the coordinating team bent on reforming the mindset of young people, my daily routine took me from slums to ghettos, old and abandoned buildings in different parts of the country. I met a diverse body of young people, all with devastating and somber stories to tell. Our dialogues aimed to evoke feedback responses from them and further proffer possible steps or ideas that, in their views, would be fruitful, thereby meeting humane standards against vices of abject poverty, injustice, corruption, and the like.

In most of our deliberations, we played recordings of various political actors and individuals in high places who expressed serious discontent with violence and the resulting consequences. Most of the politicians on tape would swiftly decline when asked if they would encourage their children or close family members to engage in violence and riotous conduct. We would use these recordings to pose the solemn question, ‚If a sitting minister is unwilling to send his or her children to engage in political violence, are you willing to take to the streets and engage in political violence that is detrimental to your life and future?' The answer has always been a resounding no!

Sadly enough, this has not been the case in the political history of our nation in all general election campaigns. There are documented cases of violence and unnecessary deaths in almost all general electoral exercises conducted thus far, as rival political parties thrive on preaching the principles of 'divide and rule'. This has inevitably suppressed and undermined the provisions found within the tenets of democratic processes. These were the kinds of situations that took up most of my time as I deepened my stance in advocacy and activism. These were opportunities to discuss relevant issues while employing a sense of humor that promotes confidence and interactive dialogue between us, the mediators, and our humble respondents, the youths.

By all leaps and bounds of our collective efforts, in one way or another, we curtailed to some extent the violent tendencies and outbursts that would have disrupted the forthcoming 2007 general elections. We constantly engaged the electronic and print media with programs that condemned the participation of youths in violence across the nation.

My exposure grew over time, and I began to note the fulfillment that comes along with servitude. One such organization is Caritas Freetown, where I started off as an Office Assistant in 2008. With the spirit of hard work and dedication, this was to change much later. After working for a few years, I was promoted to Program Manager in 2013. As the saying goes in geography, 'the higher you climb up, the cooler it becomes'.

However, working for non-profit organizations is a different ball game and is in complete contrast to this geographic allusion. My ascension, though well-earned, came with a lot of upbeat sacrifices during my early inclusion into the fold. I was dedicated to my social circles, and I became directly or indirectly involved in almost all projects that the organization had by then. While I received no financial rewards in most of these endeavors, my primary goal was to learn in-depth about social work and capacitate myself in something that I passionately loved doing.

After becoming Programs Manager for a few months, I came into contact with a wonderful lady who impacted my life greatly. She had been directed to me to conduct interviews as she was in Freetown doing research on the democratic processes in the country, as well as the participation of faith-based institutions in humanitarian actions. Her interviews and discussions further deepened my knowledge and provided much insight into the rudiments involved in working for non-profit organizations.

At the end of her last interview with me, we had a lengthy private discussion where she informed me that it would be wonderful to apply for a course in humanitarian studies at Fordham University in the United States of America. She insisted that it was a course designed for professionals and that it would be worthy of a try.

After giving it much thoughtful consideration, it became an opportunity to broaden my horizons, and I applied for a diploma in Humanitarian Assistance. I was fortunate to be admitted to Fordham University, where I graduated with an excellent result. This was made possible by the Healey International Relief Foundation and the University Administration through one of their acclaimed teachers who became more like a sister, Dr. Melissa Labante, and Brendan Cahill, the Director of the Institute of International Humanitarian Assistance.

Reading journals, articles, and projects based on related disciplines helped broaden my horizons. I acquired a lot of knowledge that helped shape and diversify my call to serving humanity. It placed me in a position to make informed judgments about various situations that came along with my job.

Upon returning home, my commitment doubled as my job description tagged me with meeting schedules, appointments, project designs, and their development. Implementation and meeting deadlines were enough to dissuade someone who lacked the passion and moral fortitude to be in my line of duty. Sometimes, situations would arise where your faith and devotion in humanity are questioned and put to the test. In some projects, you encounter so much criticism and ingratitude from those you seem to spend endless time alleviating their situations, even after your most sincere and selfless indulgence. But when you embark on a journey that is passion-driven, even the most fearful impediments become fun and feats to overcome. The nature and context of my call are one of selflessness, and as I worked in one community after another, from one organization to the next, my interactions deepened and blossomed with time as I improved my propensity to establish sincere and long-lasting relationships.

This has been the bedrock of the many successes I have attained thus far. For many who have had personal encounters with me, exploring the chances to strengthen bonds with others has always been my fundamental principle in life. Humility, honesty, and the spirit of "Ubuntu," a Zulu phrase that literally means unity and love for one another, guide me. This is not to speak against precautionary measures that deal with integrity and establishing personal boundaries, but to implore an inner instinct in attending to the core values that uphold the dignity of oneness to which nature and the universe bind us.

Focus and commitment, whatever pursuit in life, is enough inspiration to give us lasting fulfillment as we play our roles in restoring the lost dignity of Mother Nature. We must be inspired to do something, be it great or small, and focus on it with a mindset to improve whatever we commit to. As we employ our collective efforts to improve the lives of others, we radiate a sense of purpose to others. And if we heed a call that serves each other with empathy, dignity, and respect, we illuminate our true selves to the endless possibilities bestowed on our paths to make our world a better place.

As a Program Manager for Caritas Freetown, I contributed immensely to educating people about the Ebola virus that ravaged my beloved Sierra Leone since we first recorded the case on May 24, 2014, which only recently emerged in Sierra Leone. I campaigned fervently to bring an end to this epidemic that claimed the lives of many Sierra Leoneans across the country. My campaigns took me to schools, churches, neighborhoods, and, at the end of each campaign, along with my team of 275 community volunteers, we donated hand sanitizers, soap, and chlorine to locals and other stakeholders.

Many people were in denial that Ebola was not real, and convincing such people was a significant challenge. Some folks would tell stories about medical personnel and the government being in league, claiming that the virus is man-made. This was especially prevalent in the early stages of the outbreak when sensitization was inadequate. Suspects/patients were taken to treatment centers, only to never be seen again by their families and friends. Stigmatization was also a major issue during the Ebola period. People were stigmatized, especially when their houses were quarantined or when family members were suspected or infected with the dreadful Ebola virus.

As an organization, we had to go through a lot to convince people. We started breathing a sigh of relief when we began counting Ebola survivors as a nation. In response to denial, we showed them films and photos of Ebola survivors, and we even presented the survivors to them.

The staff of Caritas Freetown, including myself, was able to support communities by providing them with food while they were quarantined, conducting contact tracing, offering psychosocial support to Ebola survivors and their families, providing additional discharge packages, and engaging in extensive community awareness raising and community engagement through religious leaders, influential community stakeholders, and many more. Partners like Healey International Relief Foundation, Caritas Germany, Manos Unidas, FADICA, Catholic Mission Australia, AGEH, to name a few, helped Caritas Freetown immensely in achieving the above humanitarian interventions.

Chapter 9

A New Dawn

Reading motivational stories from real life has greatly touched and inspired me to persevere when faced with never-ending obstacles. After all the struggle and effort, one employs during their challenging moments, they can always sigh with relief, knowing they are not alone. Others have encountered turbulent waters on their paths, yet they have managed to rise above such difficulties and correct their mistakes, earning the applause of humanity.

One of the first actions I took when I was with NMJD in the role of a Youth Animator was to assist in coordinating the visit of British students volunteering with Christian Aid UK. These students were evaluating a project funded by Christian Aid UK. I was tasked with being their tour guide and helping them delve into the research work they came to conduct. This interaction proved valuable as it provided an opportunity to gain diverse viewpoints on youth activism, expanding not only my network but also broadening my horizons.

In a nutshell, I learned a lot from these students. I came to understand that people hold varying opinions on youth issues and their vital role in a nation's development landscape. In Sierra Leone, despite its challenges, which is known as the most religiously tolerant country in the world, Muslims and Christians coexist under the same roof and engage in many common activities. Interfaith marriages, brotherly and sisterly relationships are profound daily practices between the two groups. Both faiths consistently make room for peace and dialogue in their endeavors.

This unity is a significant motivating factor for religious or faith-based organizations that are dedicated to making Sierra Leone a better place. In times of humanitarian crisis, these organizations come together to alleviate the plight of ordinary Sierra Leoneans. The doors of churches, mosques, temples, and faith-based organizations are always open to those in need, distributing emergency supplies that can save lives. This unity was clearly demonstrated after the brutal war, the Ebola outbreak, and the 2017 flood and mudslide that struck Freetown.

After serving for three years with NMJD, I changed jobs and joined another Non-Governmental Organization in 2007, the Centre for the Coordination of Youth Activities (CCYA), as a Program Assistant.

A significant portion of my job description involves advocacy, youth mobilization, drafting projects, seeking prospective donors and partners, and further interacting with donors (corporate, institutional, and individual funders) to understand their interest in the scope of the project frame. The routine and expectations extend to providing budget breakdowns, expected project time frames, implementation, and deadlines.

My new job exposed me to an extensive mix of people with varied academic and social backgrounds. Without any expectations about my mettle, my colleagues ensured that I was pleasantly surprised, as I appeared too humble to learn from them. My role was well-defined, and my humility and proactiveness provided enough leverage to fit into the larger scheme of things. Learning more about programming was a significant step I had to embark on, as I was expected to carry out evidence-based advocacy, engage with government ministries and agencies, learn how to source donors, plan events, develop proposals, conduct site visits to youth groups in slums, ghettos, and shanty communities, and develop new methods of donor engagement, among other tasks. Initially, I anticipated that it would take me over five months to fully grasp the details, but with sufficient mentoring and dedication, it took just under two months to firmly grasp my job specifications.

As I became grounded in my job, my opportunities increased. I must acknowledge that while serving in my present job, I also worked part-time with both the Women's Refugee Commission, where I served as a Youth Adviser in the Out of School Youth Initiative Program, and as a National Incident Coordinator for the National Electoral Watch (NEW), a civil society organization focused on monitoring national elections.

However, once I settled into the routine, I began to enjoy every minute spent within the confines of my job. I was exposed to numerous international travel opportunities in different countries within Africa and Europe. My job wasn't limited to Youth Advocacy and Programming alone; I participated in various workshops, seminars, and conferences on capacity building, both at home and abroad, from time to time.

In my pursuit of excellence, I was part of the advocacy team that actively campaigned for the establishment of the National Youth Commission (NYC). As I aim to make more strides in humanitarian activism, I wholeheartedly said goodbye to CCYA in 2009 after serving for two years and joined Caritas Freetown as a Project Manager.

Working for Caritas Freetown, I was initially involved in a life skills project with school kids from different communities. Working with kids can be quite fascinating as they are capable of transmitting so much uninhibited love and respect that it can sometimes be overwhelming. Teaching them the basic strategies guiding us to adapt to the various changes that come with their childhood development, and sensing their eagerness to learn, took me back to my school days and left me pondering why I wasn't as excited as them.

There were moments that touched my heart more deeply than anything I had ever felt. Working with kids made me even more humble than before. It also made me realize that educating young minds meant more to me than just keeping busy; it became, as they say, my passion, and the thought itself was self-gratifying. Reflecting on each day I spent with the kids filled my heart with joy, appreciation, and left a lasting impression on my memory. Initially, it required a lot of patience to sit with them and help them understand concepts using the simplest possible terms, as it's better to explain to kids using multiple examples and illustrations.

But gradually, we overcame all these barriers, and it became a much more enjoyable experience. Kids are very innocent; they shower you with so much love and affection. I had already started feeling attached to these beautiful souls who always smiled while talking to you. I was already feeling blessed and humbled to get an opportunity to spend time with them and make a difference in their lives. Even though I worked there for a short span of time, we bonded so well and made a small impact on each other's lives. I can assure you that children have brilliant ideas about what they want to become in life, but they need inspiration to pursue their dreams. I gave them what I could afford: knowledge to help them achieve greatness.

My promotion from Project Manager to Program Manager in the following two years didn't come as a surprise, as my loyalty to serving humanity paid off sooner than expected. Personally, what brings me real pleasure and pride isn't making six-figure salaries, but rather giving hope and comfort to an Ebola survivor, a child orphaned by the just-ended Ebola epidemic, or transforming a malnourished child into a healthy boy who can lead a fulfilling life on his own. As the saying goes, „The beauty of life doesn't depend on personal achievements but on how many smiles you can bring to others' faces."

Due to my dedicated contributions to the service of humanity, I was part of a research program titled „Living in the Past," organized by a research group called the Humanitarian Policy Group. I also served as the Board Chair for the Initiative for Children and Youth Initiatives and recently as a Board Member at ENCISS. The Program Board's role is to provide advice to the ENCISS team, approve grants recommended by the Grants Sub Committee, and support the program's aims.

By 2012, I had been appointed as the In-Country Manager for the Healey International Relief Foundation (HIRF) and later as the official Spokesperson. I continue to serve in these three capacities to this day. The Healey International Relief Foundation, established in 2001, is a 501(c)3 public charity under US law, aiming to improve the quality of life for vulnerable individuals and families in deprived nations. Sierra Leone, a country affected by civil war and adverse socioeconomic conditions, was just the right place to be. The Foundation's focus on Sierra Leone and its people was the dynamic inspiration of the late Monsignor Daniel Sullivan.

Monsignor Sullivan formed a close friendship and bond with the Archbishop of Sierra Leone, Joseph Ganda, after the end of the eleven-year civil war that ravaged the country. This friendship brought two forces together to shine a light on a country few had ever heard of. This friendship led the Healey family to learn about the plight of this West African country and the brutalities committed against its people, especially women and children.

HealeyIRF implemented some of its first projects in the country: St. Mary's Home for Children, St. Stephen's Home for Amputees, and Serabu Hospital. Currently, HealeyIRF supports the Charity Health Network, orphan and vulnerable children's programs, medical supplies and donations, and socioeconomic and community development initiatives.

The journey has been incredibly rich in intricate experiences, particularly for someone who has encountered the widest spectrum of circumstances. Reflecting upon this transformation, from youth to adulthood, from a participant in conflict to a champion of compassion, from a seeker of guidance to a provider of counsel, from a recipient of support to a source of support, it becomes evident that maintaining faith in the potential of tomorrow paves the path to achievement.

CHAPTER 10

Life's Lessons: Food for Thought

At times, people utter words to you at just the right moment, words that can bring about everlasting positive changes in your life. It could be seen as a coincidence, or perhaps it's all part of a greater plan.

I prefer to believe that every individual you encounter in life serves a purpose. Each person imparts a lesson, regardless of its magnitude. The preceding sections have extensively covered my journey from humble beginnings to a more fortunate state, and the unwavering determination that helped me overcome the challenges of my early formative years.

Now, I kindly ask for your indulgence as I share my experiences regarding the guiding principles that have shaped my life until this point. My hope is that these principles will resonate with you, bringing warmth and blessings to your hearts.

Guiding Principles in Life:

- The pull of gravity
- Physical Boundaries
- Choices and decisions
- Fear of failure
- Loss of purpose
- Unbelief in God

The Pull of Gravity:

"It is easy to fall than rise,
easier to break than make,
easiest to fail than succeed"

Gravity, as my science teacher used to say, is a force that attracts objects in space towards each other. On Earth, it pulls them towards the center, right to the ground. The English scholar would have this to add, rendering gravity a more serious term as it refers to the seriousness of something considered in terms of its unfavorable consequences. Other synonyms that will include solemnity and seriousness in somebody's attitude or behavior.

As we strive to succeed in our various spheres of vocation, we must hasten to note the existence of an innate force that always tends to pull us back, no matter how much awareness or ignorance we apply to it. This force, though abstract, is serious, solemn, and also wields authority and control if we ignore or fail to take steps that would mitigate its effects. Attached to this force are the sudden and abstract feelings of lassitude, the transience of human life, the effects of procrastination, and the open challenges that shape us towards our goals, a few among the dozens
.

Keep your focus on the summit:

"Eyes are for sights, minds are for visions"

Life is a gift for humanity to embrace. Some folks were born poor, deaf, blind, but that does not mean it is the end of their story. The route to greatness is never smooth; one has to go through a lot in life. Do not ever allow people to define you. Every human being has a drop of greatness.

Do not ever give up on your dreams! As a child, teen or adult, you should remember have this on your mind that you were not part of the decision to be what you are. You can only be a part of it when you fail to accept and make the positive change. Philippians 4:6 – "Be anxious (careful) for nothing!" This is sufficient enough.

Through a divine blueprint, everyman was destined for a purpose; which makes it more thoughtful to point out the fact that destiny is determined by men, and purpose by our creator. Reaching our destiny is an earnest process that entails our active participation throughout our tenure of living. This involves what we do or engage in. Failing to meet our summits mostly result from ignorance which is a stealthy and abstract enemy that could only be dispelled by knowing our purpose! In finding out about our purpose, it is important that we at all times keep a slow, sure and a steady faith in whatever aspiration or calling that we have or perceive.

At birth, every child would struggle to open its eyes to let us know they should always be kept open; and this certainly requires some amount of effort from our part. Every desire or purpose should be pursued with a wide gaze and a fixed scope of view. Keeping a constant and focused view will greatly influence our perception, especially when we do it with a positive attitude and actions that are geared towards that.

Granted that nature has provided in abundance the possibilities needed to meet our desires, it is but thoughtful that we play our roles with an unscathed manner and matching attitude. As we pass each day under the open skies, our focuses are altered, mostly by our experiences (good or bad). In order to deliver the best, an actor needs to master his role, through effective commitment, practice and a fixed gaze.

This can also be compared to the way we tune our minds, aligning them with the perception of our true calling. Just as actors assume specific roles, we too must strive to fulfill our roles with a clear aim of reaching the pinnacle of success. However, achieving our goals doesn't mean we can ignore the challenges we must juggle, particularly in the face of evolving trends.

In the midst of the world's rapid technological progress, various complex situations have emerged that signify a shift in the prevailing norms. These technological advancements have brought together unexpected challenges—ranging from climate change and conflicts to political and economic turmoil, natural disasters, and even our own self-centered desires. These factors underline the importance of maintaining unwavering focus and determination as we work towards our most cherished objectives.

By consistently renewing our focus amidst the unfolding challenges and maintaining a steady perspective on the goals we choose to pursue, we can embody the essence of accomplishing our destined purpose in life. This process can serve as a guiding principle leading us towards fulfillment.

Self-Discipline:

"When we discipline ourselves, we define ourselves"

Self-discipline is doing what we ought to do even without encouragement from others. Counted to be one of the greatest attributes, self-discipline is a crucial aspect, especially for all who go through the transiting phases of childhood and adulthood. Both developmental stages are strategic, can be influenced and more so factored in a giant pincer by the evolutionary concepts, and to a greater degree constitute our personal demeanor. Studies have shown that child bearing and rearing is a two-way street that entails a great amount of discipline. Having gone through the phases of childhood, certain characteristic traits, learned or acquired will pave to the latter life we lead. Suffice it to say what we turn out to be at age 50 can be directly correlated to what we do in our teens.

As a tip, using motivational keys such as confidence, perseverance, courage et al, we could coin a much convenient attitude to cope with through the spiraling years. There is no such person that can motivate, encourage or inspire you, better than you can. Simply put, we bear a greater share, both in angle and dimension to whatever mode of inspiration or motivation others could offer. It is clearly obvious that we pick up inspiration or the spur to do from others, but it is also incumbent on us to modify and make the best of it. No one can motivate or encourage you better than yourself, the same manner no one can discipline you better than you can.

When we discipline ourselves, the following outcomes are sure: we define boundaries (set standards, mostly using a mentor); we face and possibly defy the effects of gravity (control the fall or fall with control); we may make enemies (a possible aspect about life); we may witness breath-taking moments (another inevitable outcome); we may experience the feeling of lassitude (this can be factored out by persistence) and we eventually soar above the force of gravity (falling) and its associated effects!

Physical Boundaries:

"Leverage your gifts and use them to achieve your dreams"

Physical boundaries and limitations can be odds in our paths if we give them full attention. This is not to imply total ignorance of their existence but the awareness that our weaknesses and impossibilities can turn out to be our advantage, if we discover and use them, amicably well. However, it takes a very high level of commitment to defy the paradoxical feelings of self-pity, open rebuke or dissuasion that overwhelm us when we pity or yield to our limitations. When we do such, we give them a total dominance over our desires and expectations. Gifts, sometimes called talents are specific to our purposes but with equal potency to make our lives comfortable and fulfilling.

The hardest part is discovering them, which requires an undiluted commitment, persistence, inspiration and deep meditation to bring out their lustrous effect. They are invigorating to our souls, with a deep sense of satisfaction, especially when we realize the source. God has given talents to all of humanity, but it takes focus and dedication to come to terms with your talents and be a useful element to the rest of humanity. Every talent, no matter how small, has the potency to defy and modify the most bewildering limitation.

Leverage Your Gifts:

Lionel Messi was diagnosed too short to play professional football. Yes, he was born with a growth defect but he didn't question his creator about his physical form. However, he made up for his lack of height with his flair and ability to play professional football. He is on record to be one of the greatest football players of our time. Born Stevland Hardaway Judkins (Stevie Wonder) is a musician, singer, songwriter, record producer, and multi-instrumentalist! He has walked the hall of fame as a distinguished personality I need not remind you that he is blind! I have made these allusions to help understand that we were made to dominate and not to be defined by our limits! Both examples are of individuals who have modified and defied physical limitations with contradictory qualities.

We were made to be the highest creation; homo sapiens-sapiens (man with intelligence) and for this reason we are given a measure of anointing, which is our ability. We are able to do and become whatever we choose if we stop making mere excuses, get out of the closet or comfort zone and strive to do and be our utmost bests! When we thrive for higher ideals, we should strive at all lengths to put a check on excuses and bring out the best in us. Excuses are loops from which stems flops, distracted priorities and the sloppy allusions of failure and mediocrity.

It must start with us, breaking those limits – with a first step! That is, discovering our potentials (purpose) while seeking guidance to make our world more colourful (destiny-fulfilled). Self-discovery is influenced by a strong desire and persistence, and mostly comes with a few tests that are both mandatory and fundamental to our significance and diversity in life. So, it actually takes the merits of odds to discover our gifts, for without odds, we are unable to use and guard our gifts well. When we use and guard our gifts with every bit of care, then we are assured of a swift climb over every limitation.

Choices and Decisions:

"Success does not consist in never making blunders but in never making it a second time"

Both – choices and decisions – are voluntary actions, meaning, they are executed with consciousness. Choice is an act of selecting between two or more possibilities or a decision to choose one thing, person, or course of action in preference to others. Decision is the act of deciding, reaching a conclusion or making a judgment or something that somebody chooses or makes up his or her mind about, after considering it and other possible choices. Put forward by the Oxford Advance Learner's dictionary, both maintained the same word in context, clearly showing there's no two-way about it! Choosing as in choice, deciding as in decision! We can make the irrevocable conclusion that we engage in both wholeheartedly; even when situations dictate.

Sometimes in life, the good decisions we make might keep our shoulders high and choices that are bad send the heads down. The inverse is also true. Whatever the outcome of the choices we make or decisions we take; it is okay, if we say so. The outcomes are better defined or modified by us; that is, how we act towards them and how we present our resolve. Our action towards the outmost wrong choice or decision determines how we get out of them. In getting out of them, it is a prerequisite to keep in mind the experiences from those wrong steps!

Choice and decision are almost executed simultaneously and there can never be a fine line between the two. However, choices are fundamental to decisions, as both have the similar translations. A positive and uplifting resolve to any situation that has been accepted by us as wrong proves to be the quickest and probably most certain way to curtail the depression attached, when we brood over the bad ones. The unbearable effects of depression outweigh the transient emotions we might experience when we own up or come to terms with our choices and decisions.

Make Calculated and Wise Choices:
"Taking calculated risks is quite different from being hasty"

One might want to ask, what does it take to do such? Well, it is simple. I'd like to share a story before divulging. The story goes off a farmer who was very hardworking and diligent in his pursuit. His crops yielded and the farming business expanded well. He had established himself from a little piece of land to owning almost a third of his town. He became the envy of all. As humans, we are prone to yield and do more. He was confident to express proposals for a bigger extension. According to him, he had outgrown his present and desired a very big one. In fact, ten times his present spot. His proposals met the ears of many who had various places to show but kept turning them down by the day.

One day, a young man from a distant town arrived and advertised a plot of land he had inherited as a legacy from his father. The farmer was thrilled by the description and entertained his proposed business partner with a sumptuous feast. In the early hours of the following day, they set off and reached the wonderful plot after a two-hour trek. It was 7:00 am, and the sun was ascending the horizon. Upon seeing the expanse of land, he heaved a sigh of relief and immediately initiated a negotiation.

„What is your price?" he inquired. The young man, quite relaxed, calmly replied, „Nothing! I am willing to let you have this plot of land for nothing." The farmer was stunned. His eyes bulged as if he had been handed a death sentence. He couldn't believe his ears. He pondered what could possibly compel this young man to give away a fortune for nothing!

He stood speechless; this land was so vast compared to the size of 160 standard football fields. He regained his composure and asked again, „Are you serious?" The young man confidently affirmed, but with a specific condition, „Yes, but only on one condition! I will give you this stick for you to mark the spot at which you want your land to end, starting from where we stand. The only thing you must return before sunset." The farmer was delighted and rejoiced at this deal. The young man reminded him that if he failed to return before sunset, he would forfeit his farm and everything he possessed. The farmer hastily agreed.

It was 7:30 am when he set off with the stick. He pranced around, contemplating the various crops he would grow. Hours passed, and it was already 12 pm. He continued to ponder, meditating on his options. By 3:30 pm, he had come quite a distance, but he had not reached a decision or made a choice. Gazing at the sky, he noticed the sun slowly setting. Realizing the time, he decided to turn back, doing so with great urgency. He ran and ran, pushing himself to his limits. At 4:30 pm, he was still running. Exhaustion and distance had taken their toll by 5:30 pm. He stopped to catch his breath and was astonished by what he saw.

I need not conclude this story...

The aforementioned tale vividly illustrates our purpose in life, along with the choices and decisions we make. The farmer viewed the stick provided for demarcation with disappointment. He contemplated the bargain, his farm, his fortunes, and how far he was from the midpoint. He couldn't afford to go back to place the stick as a landmark, nor could he afford to lose all he had toiled for. Nevertheless, he had agreed to the bargain. He was shocked to discover he had lost everything. Ultimately, he couldn't bear the shock, and he dropped dead.

Let's draw parallels between the farmer's story and our lives. The plot of land symbolizes the world; the farmer represents humanity; the stick signifies our purpose; the young man embodies chance or a benefactor; the purpose of the trip reflects our destiny.

When we take a chance in life, we make choices, decisions, and eventually effect changes. By every estimation, we always hope to get the best out of every choice or decision we make. To get the best, we need to involve an arbitrary guide to help us walk the necessary path – this is when we seek guidance, mostly divine, to help us on our journey. This is where God takes over, in the same manner a young benefactor would, had the farmer requested it. Naturally, a plot of such description (akin to the world) can hardly ever be managed or secured alone. When we communicate our choices to God, regardless of the outcome, He becomes involved. You may go round and round, but you may never go wrong! We can relate this to the experiences we face each day – choosing and deciding.

When faced with an opportunity to make a choice, we are also confronted with anxiety, sometimes mixed with fear and perplexity, all of which work together to sway us. If we fail to seek divine guidance, the result is a miscarriage of visions and well-brooded plans, simply failing to acknowledge the effects and the owner of time. The simple fact is that time is indispensable, waits for no one, and chiefly defines the circadian rhythm (day and night, sleep and wake, birth and death, every day...); it is wise to recognize its owner. The owner of time is best positioned to determine its use. As in the unfortunate case of the farmer, he was carried away by the many prospects we consider enjoying in life, without considering the purpose for which we were designed and the unexpected surprises that lie ahead.

The insatiable Adamic nature within us always longs and yearns for more. When we are given more, we cannot make use of it all but must exercise our decision-making prowess. As the farmer pranced forward, he planned to the extent of ignoring the purpose of his trip, much like how we sometimes overlook the purpose of our lives. Every person has been given this same opportunity: the farmer, the human; the stretch of land, the world! By ignoring his mandate (reason for being) and mantle (guiding principles – our gifts, or props... to keep us on stage), the farmer met his grave loss.

We are born into this world by virtue of choices and decisions. As children of the universe, we should be mindful of making choices or decisions that our subconscious minds will later appreciate – whether they are good, bad, made from dictation or impulse. Such choices should be interpreted by our responses, which in most cases should be positive. While we are often quick to adapt to good outcomes, we should also be prepared to acknowledge and learn from the bad and ugly outcomes with a positive mindset. Failing to recognize the negative outcomes is the most daring part; this realization comes with pain and embarrassment.

Another common fact is that most of the wrong decisions or choices we make come with an impulsive and electrifying effect. This effect rapidly takes over the mind and influences our mood thereafter, resembling the effects associated with listlessness. The power of dominance exhibited by negative outcomes is far greater and lasts longer than those experienced after positive outcomes. Just as in our various vocations, it's important to be cautious in the choices we make and the decisions we stick to. However, a mystifying force, which often speaks to our inner selves, soft in nature and not easily swayed by heroic actions, provides a better brake for any choice we make. Mostly, good choices, decisions, or outcomes are mainly rooted in an evaluated and sequential thought pattern. Connecting with a benefactor and deity, such as God, involves a surge of patience that develops over time, not suddenly.

From the moment we invite God into the equation, we find ourselves embraced by a tranquil and serene assurance, allowing us to harmonize with His intentions. This audacious journey is accompanied by the confidence that He holds the power to transform unfavorable outcomes into something better. Cultivating a faith-centered outlook while engaging and patiently awaiting His response adds a profound layer of determination to our decision-making. It's worth noting that the solutions we fervently seek often manifest amidst the quietude of our thoughts, urging us to adopt an unwavering stance infused with positivity. This is the juncture at which we courageously embark on the quest to attune ourselves to the gentle imprints in our hearts, seeking our validation to validate their efficacy.

Avoid Silent Killers:

"Do not wallow in the mud of pain"

Silent killers are personal issues we regret so badly and at times feel too shy or embarrassed to share with others. They get stocked by the day, and keep growing in all forms until they become a huge burden to carry. Maybe, something happened in the past that always send chills to your spine whenever it pops up. It is okay to have reflections but never allow them to dominate you. Man is a spirit. This is why our mood can be affected by various circumstances, and not our destinies. When such thoughts get to us, we must appreciate and start turning them into positives. They actually happened at instances to bless others and not to destroy us. No matter how despicable the circumstance or situation might have been, do not wallow in self-pity whenever you reflect on them.

When you wallow in regret or pity over your bad pasts, you gradually end up with depression which eats up all feelings of happiness and you are left with nothing but sadness, low self-esteem, poor concentration, sleeplessness, and even to the extent of killing oneself. Imagine how much we cater for when we allow silent killers to take over us! Whenever bad feelings get to our minds, we should welcome and refer to them in prayers. We can turn any feeling our situation into a happy one; by simply searching our depths, turning the tides by maintaining a positive mental attitude. By doing such, repeatedly, we can also buy comfort and happiness, at a cheaper cost too.

Studies have proven that no amount of happiness can be achieved without a prior construction in the mind. This is to let us know that happiness can only be found within ourselves. If we cannot find it in ourselves, it is clearly impossible to find it elsewhere. These unpleasant feelings (silent killers) will lighten up until they completely wad off like a mist when we refer them to God. Tell Him all, He can surely keep a secret. Don't tell men …!!!

Avoid Double Standards:

"If you don't stand for something you fall for nothing"

People with double standards are Janus-faced. According to Roman mythology, Janus, the god of beginnings, of the past, future and peace, amongst others, was traditionally depicted as having two faces by virtue of having two heads on one body. The heads were joined at the pane of the neck, which allowed him to see both ways. Double standards equally mean double attitudes, double personalities and so on. Choose to be what you are without compromising your integrity. Our physical behavior in one way or the other makes up our personality and also aids the perception of others about us. It is important to stand up for what we believe or represent; put your foot down for this and do it without any form of malice.

The human personality and reputation are embedded and mostly recognized as one trait; thus we ought to treat both our outward and inward presentation with every bit of cognizance. Our spirits reflect and portray our images. The image we put on is the physical translation of our spirit. Joy, pain, victory, defeat all stem from our spirit and relay to other mortals through the physical images they see. This image also constitutes our habits, which is what others see and physically relate with. For most people, having double standards is fun, adventurous and make them think they are good at it, but only for a short while!

Playing the Blame Game – Why me?

"Appreciate God by accepting situation"

Stop playing the blame game! Oh God! Why me? When we are faced, with a quest or situation, ask yourself; 'Is it me?' before asking; 'Why me?' You might be faced with a particular situation or a perennial circumstance which needs to be addressed by only you. It is up to us to gather together every courage and strength to face the challenges attached to our quest or situation. This might in no way be simple and the element will be connecting your faith and believing in yourself. Changing any situation requires steady dedication on our part and comes through patience and persistence. If we are determined for a change, believe in a change, work towards a change, we will definitely bring a change.

The power to change any situation lies within us – acceptance is the first step; determination the second and faith is the final and greatest element. Waste no time in asking 'why?', but rather spend much time in gratitude with thanksgiving; this automatically attracts His attention. In all situations, the bible admonishes us to thank God in appreciation! He knows best and why He said so. Definitely you know yesterday and hopefully today, but you dare not tell the future! We scarcely have a glimpse into the future. Be determined to change any given situation by asking Him in prayers to guide and better your decisions.

Enroll in the School of Mistakes:

*"The most intractable mistake
is better than never trying"*

*"Make your own mistakes
and learn your own lessons"*

The school of mistake is compulsory for everyone to attend. Records have proven that most successful people have make blunders; some of them have made uncountable errors that turn out to be testimonies. The tuition fee is free but I bet you'll graduate with honors if only you do two things whilst in session; be focused and be determined!

Let us refer to what we enjoy today – the light bulb. Thomas Edison was the first scientist to discover the filament light bulb. He made two thousand attempts and failed two thousand times! In one of his interviews, he was asked how he felt about failing to make the light bulb work after two thousand trials. This was his reply 'I did not fail two thousand times to make the light bulb work, I discovered two thousand ways not to make a light bulb work.' From his mistakes, he graduated with honors to produce the light bulb.

Making mistakes doesn't guarantee failure. Actually, it's quite the opposite. Mistakes are an important part of our paths to success. The journey to a successful life doesn't exclude errors or setbacks. Success has its own chances for mistakes and failures, which often turn out to be important for achieving great things. These experiences help us stay concentrated and committed to learning from our own lessons. We shouldn't let our mistakes destroy our dreams.

Fear of Failure:

*"Always recognize your three Fs –
your flops, failures and fumbles"*

Fear which also means to be afraid of, to be frightened, to worry about, to be terrified of, is basically an unpleasant feeling caused by the possibilities of danger, pain, threat, etc. You don't need this feeling and must fight it with every bit of might. When you are afraid of failure or open to rebuke then you are not ready to be positioned for the rebound. Our creator liberally gave us the ability to deal with fear as recorded in his word; 'God has not given us the spirit of fear, but of love, power and a sound mind'. 3 humble facts to know about failure:

Everyone Fails:

- Don't count yourself out; you are meaningful.

No One Enjoys Failure

- Key yourself to learn from your failures and bring the best out of them.

Response to Failure Is Different

- Failure is a weapon. As ironic as it sounds, failure is a weapon of self-resurrection and not self-destruction.

There are two attributes of failure: You either *fail forward or you fail backward. When you fail forward the following outcomes are possible:* you learn lessons; you discover yourself; you accept and appreciate and you become an achiever. *When you fail backward the following are possible:* you make excuses; you blame others, including yourself; you respond negatively and you become an avenger. Do not fear to fail but fail to fear!

Fear serves as the stage upon which adversaries and detractors thrive, as it constitutes a central element within their strategy to assert dominance and manipulate our thought patterns. Their intention is to confine us within a state of desolation and denial, fostering a host of negative emotions that undermine the essence of our purpose. Similar to Lucifer or Satan, who lost his divine grace and now harbors jealousy towards the grace we presently experience, these forces work vigorously to pull humanity down. Their tactic often involves unraveling our past mistakes, causing us to doubt our worth and succumb to fear.

When fear takes hold of us, the adversary capitalizes on this vulnerability, undermining our faith and thereby estranging us from God's favor. Faith and fear are stark contrasts – faith propels us forward with enthusiasm, while fear cripples us. The former uplifts and inspires, whereas the latter diminishes and fades away. Faith pleases our inner conscience, an essential element in manifesting our fervent aspirations. It's vital not to allow fear to erode the divine grace that empowers us to seek our desires and receive blessings before their realization in heaven.

Our essential needs have been ordained long before our conception by our Creator. It's natural to encounter setbacks; indeed, there is much wisdom to be gleaned from failures. The true triumph in life lies not in avoiding falls but in consistently rising each time we stumble. To achieve this, it's imperative to possess a sound mind within a healthy body. Embrace your failures, extract valuable lessons from them, and seize control over your world.

Make No Room for Complacency:

- "A little sleep, a little slumber brings poverty"

When we strive to make the difference, we should be ready to do what it takes. A complacent life settles and functions within a particular domain. This doesn't imply that complacent people are not successful, but merely to reiterate the fact that when you carry a vision, purpose or pursuit; maybe the exceptional person you want to become or things you want to do, you have to make a lot of sacrifices. When you step out of your comfort zone for higher ideals, the universe supports you in every way. It showers you with various experiences, disciplines and values to make your purpose or pursuit, a calling. These are the blueprints of a fulfilled life, and we must certainly take them in order to stand out. This starts with you breaking the boundaries and avoiding comfort zones.

A curious and innovative mind is a restless one – always willing to push the limits. Humans are the most curious and innovative of all God's creation. With that sense, it is always wise to push more, attempt more and rise above the horizon. Our creator has constantly evolved to be the best innovator, and likewise, in His image, we must emulate the same. This claim is systematic and has been confirmed by the modern man – upright, smart and intelligent, dubbed, 'Homo Sapiens'! This is just enough to suggest that God is non-complacent, and we must do the same as His image. When we move from complacency, we are positioned for an anticipation that is rooted to our labor and attentiveness.

When I first started putting ideas to write my autobiography, I had to sacrifice time which is of extreme importance and I was having sleepless nights writing and typing page after page, spending less time with family, and in the morning, I had to make myself very fit for work at the office.

Unexpectedly, in the midst of these, I received news of the demise of my dear mum. The death of my mum on December 9 2016 was the most painful moment of my life. After God, she gave me all I need in order to live a successful life. She was the most courageous woman I have ever known. I still remember, amidst hard times, she stood firm and ensure that I see the light at the end of the tunnel. I could hardly bear the pain when the claws of death snatched her away from me. Till date, I had to shed tears bitterly upon thinking of the good and bad times we have spent together. Rest in Peace Mama!

Leverage Emerging Innovations:

"Before it was the typewriter, now it is the computer. Just so you know, tomorrow will always be better and technology is up for a rebound"

The dynamics of the world is changing by every thick of a clock. The mobile phone and the internet, for example are wonderful inventions that have brought geographical distances to just a click of the button. It is important that we upgrade our lives and keep abreast with unfolding events. Thankfully, history made it clear that humans evolved from the Old Stone Age, the Middle Stone Age to the Metal Age. I am sure this has been modified and taken to another level, the 'Mental Age' pioneered by great minds. Don't be left out! Today precedes tomorrow. Leveraging today's inventions, prepares you for tomorrow's adventures, especially the mind-blowing ones. Innovations and inventions are constantly changing with the passage of time; therefore, upgrading our lives with each invent will be a good and productive idea in this era.

Loss of Purpose – (Why Am I Here …?)

"Always define yourself … If you do, God will qualify you, if you don't, men will nullify you"

Many have wandered through life unsure of their purpose and skeptical about their destiny. They have turned round and round, hoping to turn back the hands of time. Time is the indispensable element that waits for no man, respects no man and also a chief component of the daily cycle of activities observed. If you fail to make use of time, time will make use of you and before you know it, you are half way to your grave.

If you find yourself somewhere, whether or not it was a circumstance that caused it, be grateful to be a child of the universe that is no lesser than the stars and trees. If you believe in fate and that you have a place in this world, stay assured! A place where you flourish, everything you do prospers, and where you recline in absolute comfort. We have made progress and have come this far. So, it's time to put on the cloak and stay committed in reaching your summit.

Don't live to please somebody:

*"The greatest secret to succeeding is spending your life in your own way.
Always be yourself and others will see you"*

Most young minds have heeded, to the dictates of parents and friends, which have affected their life in so many ways. We should allow them to have a say in our lives but not to define our lives. We should take responsibility for what we become in life. One should have the power to say no! When it means no!

By seeking His (God) guidance in prayers, He responds in various forms to our requests (in dreams, visions etc.).

When we are born into this world, we never determined our parents, continent, religion, and the rest of things, but there is one thing for sure – what you become in life is your responsibility. Don't allow people to drag you down. The likes of Nelson Mandela, Barack Hussein Obama, Helen Keller, etc., never allowed people to write them off. Today, they are inspirational figures to the rest of mankind. You have what it takes to be at the top!

Don't Run the Rat Race:

*"The pursuit of happiness is not a race.
Starting early does not imply finishing first;
neither does starting late imply finishing last"*

The rat race is a way of life in which everybody competes fiercely to be more successful than other. Success is a desire and everyone wants to succeed. The question is 'How to succeed?' Should we work ourselves out … and spend our lives visiting hospitals? Should we go beyond the limits and have regrets we are unable to live with?

You might engage in a small business, career or vocation. The benefits could be appalling; the profits could be very limited and unattractive … Tarry! You are on track. The fact that the benefits or profits are minimal is an indication that they will be maximal. Be determined and invest your time, energy, finance, and be consistent. Positive results are sure to come in bountiful folds.

Don't worry about others achieving great heights. Remember, it's important for chickens to stay close to the ground while eagles soar above. Imagine if chickens flew too high—what would happen to chicken soup and eggs? We all know how much our bodies need protein, and eggs are an easy and common source of it. That's why I suggest that no matter how you view your small career, job, or business, it's valued and important to the people who support you, whether in a small or big community. So, stay patient, take things slowly, and remain humble, and you'll definitely make progress!

Meet Your Real Self:

"Self-realization is the best and sincerest form of recognition"

We have finally arrived after a long journey, figuring out the guiding principles of life and subsequently defying all odds and consequently discovering ourselves – our weaknesses and strengths. We just slammed after a long trail, just to discover you! Welcome and thank you for staying with me! I'd like you to:

Meet the real you

A powerful factor to becoming oneself has to do with you, taking the first step!

Rediscover the enthusiasm of your childhood

The dreams you had as a teen (early or late), even those shattered by the circumstances of life should not define you, and you just have to move on …

Give something back:

This is important in life. You should learn to help others, even if it's just a song, a story, advice, or helping the poor and needy. You can also give uplifting messages to those who are struggling and be loyal. No act of giving is too small for society. Keep giving until the end of your life. Remember that what we give can't compare to what Mother Earth gives – she's the biggest giver.

One of her great gifts is time and space. As humans, we use her time and space effectively, expe-riencing the highs and lows from morning till night.

Set your dreams on fire and keep them burning:

Determination is a motivating factor in this life. As much as you are determine, you should have the positive mental attitude towards what you want to be in life.

Honor God with your life:

This is the greatest legacy of all times! In whatever you do, you should always have time for God Almighty. He is the Alpha and Omega, the Owner of time, the Rock of Ages …

Belief in God:

Various fields of study and disciplines have tried to provide explanations for a lot of questions (mysteries) that have pondered generations. This is the most important aspect in our journey to self-discovery. It is obviously clear that certain things exist beyond our understanding, to which the term 'supernatural events or subjects of life' adequately describes. The supernatural refers to a phenomenon that cannot be explained by science, arts or reasoning. Though we may suggest points to form a base, certain concepts exist far beyond the human mind. Such are the mysteries of life, for which to urge to suggest that a 'force – omnipotent, omnipresent and omniscient' exists in nature.

We have gone round and round, and with a very strong conviction, that there is a God! The above instances have been cited to unveil the shade of doubt plus the mist of unbelief that might have caused you to question His existence. He uses foolish things to confound the wise. He is Wisdom and cannot be outdone. Though He has raised men to give explanations in all fields of life, He unmistakably chose to hide some things in a mystery. You should not have doubt that there is a creator for the Heavens and the Earth. He is God and He lives in you!

I couldn't possibly bring this chapter to a close without sharing a crucial piece of advice with today's youth. The message is clear: don't linger on the sidelines waiting for opportunities to magically appear. Dive into the process, become an architect of your journey from the very start. Remember, monumental accomplishments often sprout from the smallest beginnings.

My own path took its initial form during my earliest days of volunteering. It was there that I sowed the seeds that later blossomed into my career. But it was my internship at NMJD that truly expanded my horizons and kindled my passion for serving humanity. It's intriguing to reflect that I began as a mere „errand boy," overcoming hurdles not with physical force, but with a blend of honesty, confidence, and relentless commitment. These virtues became the cornerstones upon which I built my recognition today. So, as you ascend towards greatness, cling to your authenticity. Shun arrogance, and remain grounded and approachable, a friend to all.

In all your pursuits, let faith be your compass, always guiding you.

Presently, I stand as a humanitarian, occupying the role of Programs Manager at Caritas-Freetown. Additionally, I've assumed the mantle of Lead Campaigner for Children's Emergency Health Needs. The drive to heal ailing children compels me beyond reason, even if it means putting my family's comfort on the line. The challenge of sourcing funds to safeguard the lives of Sierra Leone's children is a daunting one, yet as a devoted humanitarian, I hold my work paramount, always prepared to rise above.

Transitioning from a former child soldier to a dedicated humanitarian, I wholeheartedly embrace this as my undeniable calling.

Dedication

I dedicate this work to all those who have endured the challenges of the civil war in Sierra Leone, including the young men and women who were unwillingly thrust into the role of child soldiers. Special gratitude is offered to God for guiding those of us who traversed this tumultuous journey without allowing our past to taint our aspirations.

This dedication also extends to my beloved late mother, Madam Aminata Yomie Tejan, my stepmother, Mrs. Isata Songowa Charles, and my late father, Abu Alfred Charles. The souls of my father and mother may find eternal peace. Additionally, I acknowledge my dear wife, Mrs. Isata Charles, who stands as my unwavering supporter and assists in organizing my scattered writings.

To my children—Mafereh, Aminata, Juju, Daniella, Kofi, Christiana, and Uril—may this work illuminate the path of their father. I also hold deep appreciation for Monsignor Dan Sullivan, who ignited the spark for sharing my narrative and even suggested the title of this endeavor. Though he departed soon after our project's inception, may his gentle soul rest in perfect peace.

Acknowledgment

First and foremost, I offer my gratitude to God and give Him the glory for bringing my dreams to fruition. Without His blessings, my life would not have held such profound meaning.

To my dearest mother, thank you. I wish you could be by my side at this moment. However, I am certain that you now rest in the embrace of Father Abraham. I hold the firm belief that we will reunite in another realm one day.

The culmination of these thoughts demanded the contribution of many helping hands to guide them to their logical conclusion. Hence, it is only wise to express my gratitude to all those unseen hands that have made the creation of this book possible.

I am sincerely indebted to Father Peter Konteh for his unwavering encouragement and support since my inception at Caritas Freetown in 2009. Dr. Elizabeth Klett ensured the translation, completion, and publication of the German version of this book. I extend my gratitude to Daniela Brotsack for her dedicated assistance in the German translation process.

Acknowledgments are due to Monsignor Dan, who has left us, as well as to Benjamin Parra, Megan Smith, Robert Healey Sr. and Jr., and all my colleagues at the Healey International Relief Foundation for their inspirational support. I must also recognize Idriss Mansaray for her continued encouragement. Special appreciation is reserved for Umaru Fofanah for his meticulous proofreading and professional design of the original English version of this project.

Lastly, my story could not be told without the unwavering support of my niece, Mrs. Christiana Zainab

Stevens. Her assistance was invaluable throughout my graduate course at Fourah Bay College, serving as the bedrock for my academic and professional journey.

To Melissa Labonte, PHD, I extend my heartfelt thanks for serving as my mentor and motivator since our initial meeting in 2012. Finally, to an amazing Sister, Ariana Oluwole who contributed refinement of the final copy of the manuscript by reviewing and editing the contents for better readability, thank you.

May God bless and reward each and every one of you.

What say my collegues and friends

Due to my passionate contributions to humanity, some of my colleagues and friends had this to say:

Wuyatta Musu Genda, Project Supervisor- Desert Flower Foundation:

Trust me, I don't know where to begin when describing a personality like Ishmael Alfred Charles. I see him as a big brother, someone I got to know around eight years ago when I joined Caritas Freetown. He is consistently cheerful and hospitable, always proactive and willing to lend a helping hand. I regard him as one of the greatest assets of Caritas Freetown.

Kumba Gando, Caritas Freetown:

Ishmeal Alfred Charles is a down to earth person. He is an excellent advocate, especially when it has to do with the healthcare of children. He is my manager in whom I am well pleased and he is ready to help whenever he is called upon. His humanitarian work has touched many lives within the country and beyond.

Eliza Sillah, Project Officer- Caritas Freetown:

Ishmeal Alfred Charles inspired me to work for Caritas Freetown because of his commitment in the service for humanity. I called him Morgan Heritage (a famous reggae musical group in Jamaica) because of his love for the group and his love for reggae music. He believes in teamwork and he is always hungry for results.

He loves his mum dearly and hardly a day goes by without him expressing one or two about his mum. He is a cheerful giver and he personally donates his finances to children in need of emergency healthcare. No matter the pressure at work, Ishmeal would always take his time to address his colleagues and all those that matter.

Idriss Gibson Mansaray, Project Manager- Caritas Freetown:

I consider Ishmeal Alfred Charles not just a colleague but a very dear brother. We always share ideas together and we always agree to disagree or disagree to agree on certain issues that surround work or country.

He met me at Caritas Freetown and now he is my senior, but yet still he is very humble and we got each other's back in our lines of duty.

Musa Kamara, Journalist – Sierra Leone News Agency (SLENA):

I first met Ishmeal Alfred Charles in one of his campaigI first met Ishmeal Alfred Charles in one of his campaigns – to save the lives of children. In my line of duty, I can admit to you that Charles as I call him is an exceptional humanitarian. He is very passionate and full of energy in the service to humanity.

Charles's door is always open for interviews and whenever I called him on phone, he ensures providing me with the deserving statements for publication. He is a true friend of the media and the grassroots.

Short Bio of Ishmeal Alfred Charles

Ishmeal Alfred Charles is not just a survivor of Sierra Leone's brutal civil war; he's a symbol of resilience. Abducted by rebels at the tender age of 9, he bore witness to unspeakable horrors. Instead of being broken, these experiences ignited a determination within him. He resolved to be a force for positive change in his community and country, aspiring to uplift rather than destroy.

Beginning his journey with the Network Movement for Justice and Development, Charles championed economic justice through the ‚Just Mining' campaign and empowered youth in the Mano River region. His path then led to the Center for Coordination of Youth Activities, where he became a driving force for youth involvement and engagement. He advocated for the voice of the young, playing a pivotal role in reshaping national youth policy and even establishing the Young Leaders Fund for HIV.

His passion for constructive participation and decision-making earned him a seat as the youth representative on the ENCISS Programmatic Board and an advisory role for the Women's Refugee Commission's „Out of School Youth Initiative program."

At present, Charles is the In-Country Program Manager Sierra Leone for the Healey International Relief Foundation. Collaborating with Caritas Freetown, he oversees and guides their joint programs. His journey of education took him from St. Edward's Primary School to the Prince of Wales and eventually to Fourah Bay College, where he studied Peace and

Conflict Studies. He further honed his expertise with a Diploma in International Humanitarian Affairs from Fordham University. In 2021, he enrolled at York St John University in the United Kingdom where has has completed his MBA in Leadership and Management.

In a critical juncture during the 2014 West Africa Ebola outbreak, Charles was called upon by the U.S. Senate. He shared the gravity of the situation, its challenges, and the heroic efforts in Sierra Leone. His heartfelt testimony resonated deeply, prompting action. Thanks to his advocacy, the U.S. Senate's decision led to the deployment of the U.S. Center for Disease Control (CDC) to the affected regions.

At the time of publishing this book, Ishmeal is actively involved with three organizations simultaneously. The Sick Pikin Project, which was initiated in 2018 by Reverend Fr Peter Konteh and Ishmeal. It has become Ishmeal's personal passion project, where he dedicates all his spare time. Alongside this, he also holds a paid position as the In-country Manager for Sierra Leone with the Healey International Relief Foundation. Additionally, Ishmeal is currently on secondment with Caritas Freetown, where he has been serving as the Programs Manager for the past 14 years, overseeing and directing all programs and projects.

Healey International Relief Foundation

The Healey International Relief Foundation (HealeyIRF) story starts with a friendship across the ocean between the late Monsignor Dan Sullivan in the U.S. and the late Archbishop of Sierra Leone, Joseph Ganda. Meeting near the end of the decade-long civil war in Sierra Leone the two set out on a mission to help those left homeless, without food, clean water, and health care. It was through this friendship the Healey family first learned about the plight of those suffering in Sierra Leone and in 2001 the foundation was established as a 501(c)3 public charity with a mission to improve the quality of life for vulnerable individuals and families in Sierra Leone. HealeyIRF's focus is on helping those most in need by strengthening the healthcare system through the Charity Health Network, community development initiatives, and capacity training, caring for vulnerable children, and providing disaster relief and recovery.

HealeyIRF is committed to developing programs jointly with local and international partners to achieve sustainable results. Our work also supports crucial Sustainable Development Goals, such as good health and well-being, quality education, no poverty, and zero hunger. The Foundation's leadership, staff, and board members bring years of experience to our work in Sierra Leone. Through combined backgrounds in business, health, government, international development, and philanthropy our team provides unique approaches and a variety of skill sets to program development.

To learn more about the Healey International Relief Foundation please check out the following website, https://hirf.net/, and social media pages where you can show your support.

https://www.facebook.com/HealeyIRF/

https://twitter.com/HealeyIRF

https://www.instagram.com/healeyirf/

https://www.youtube.com/channel/UCQjebKI0d8etqBsVoFp30NA

Email inquiries: info@healeyphilanthropic.org

Newsletter https://lp.constantcontactpages.com/su/hQQ2ONG/scarstostars

Caritas Freetown

Caritas Freetown is a not-for-profit faith-based non-governmental organization that serves as the coordinating office for humanitarian relief and development work of the Catholic Archdiocese of Freetown in Sierra Leone. Established in 1981 by the mandate of the Catholic Bishops Conference of Sierra Leone, Caritas Freetown has been the relief and development arm of the Archdiocese for over 33 years.

The mission of Caritas Freetown is to promote integral human development, allowing people in the most disadvantaged communities to flourish and live in peace and dignity. The organization is committed to ensuring responsible and sustainable management of the natural environment for the benefit of all.

Caritas Freetown envisions a peaceful Sierra Leone characterized by solidarity and justice, where poverty is eradicated, and every citizen has access to essential needs such as healthy food, drinking water, medical care, education, justice, employment, and decent shelter. The organization strives for a world where all human beings can live with dignity, achieve holistic development, and communities are empowered to shape their own success.

The work of Caritas Freetown focuses on the Western Area Urban and Rural Districts of Sierra Leone, addressing issues of poverty, corruption, injustice, equality, good governance, peace, human rights, and empowerment of women, youth, and disabled individuals. The organization is involved in various actions related to livelihoods, relief, rehabilitation, and healthcare delivery, aiming for the holistic development of individuals.

As a Catholic Church entity, Caritas Freetown upholds strong commitment to Christian values and principles. The organization prioritizes the formation of youth groups, the promotion of family life, and the demonstration of leadership in fostering respect for the dignity and rights of every person, regardless of their religion, race, or tribe. Caritas Freetown collaborates with communities, government ministries, departments, agencies, local and international partners, and community-based organizations to build their capacities and enhance livelihoods, enabling them to address their own issues effectively.

With its extensive experience, commitment to justice and peace, and adherence to national and international laws and documents, Caritas Freetown implements projects aligned with themes such as post-war recovery, youth empowerment, family life, community development, and the promotion of human rights.

By supporting Caritas Freetown, donors contribute to the organization's efforts in eradicating poverty, promoting justice and peace, empowering marginalized groups, and building resilient communities in Sierra Leone.

Email: caritasfreetown@gmail.com
Ph: +23276175238 or +23276722736
Facebook: https://www.facebook.com/caritas.freetown/

Sick Pikin Project

The Sick Pikin (Babies) Project was established exclusively for charitable and humanitarian purposes, helping poor and sick children by raising money through campaigns and street begging to help them go through needed surgeries to make them healthy and strong again. The main aim is to cater to sick children between the ages of 0-16 years whose parents are challenged financially and cannot afford to pay the medical bills for their children. Children that are having severe medical conditions that cannot be treated here in Sierra Leone and a few minor conditions that are treated here in Sierra Leone but from extremely poor families.

Email: sikpikin@gmail.com
website: www.sickpikin.org
Sick Pikin SL Mobile and Whatsapp Number:
+23276722736
Sick Pikin UK: +448716445894
Sick Pikin US: +1973 432 6822

https://www.facebook.com/sickpikin

PLEASE SEE DETAILS ON HOW TO RECEIVE USD FROM ABROAD THROUGH VISTA BANK LTD SIERRA LEONE.

Please pay: VISTA BANK (SL) LTD
SWIFT CODE: FSTISLFR
THROUGH: CROWN AGENTS BANK
LONDON, ENGLAND

Content

Humble Beginnings	8
The Rising Tide	20
Eclipsing the Odds	26
Education for Transformation	44
Standing Tall to Life's Challenges	50
Turning Scars into Stars	56
At the Behest of a Call	64
Being Human in Humanity	72
A New Dawn	82
Life's Lessons: Food for Thought	90
The Pull of Gravity:	91
Keep your focus on the summit:	92
Self-Discipline:	94
Physical Boundaries:	96
Leverage Your Gifts:	97
Choices and Decisions:	99
Make Calculated and Wise Choices:	101
Avoid Silent Killers:	106
Avoid Double Standards:	108
Playing the Blame Game – Why me?	109
Enroll in the School of Mistakes:	110
Fear of Failure:	111
Everyone Fails:	*111*
No One Enjoys Failure	*111*
Response to Failure Is Different	*111*
Make No Room for Complacency:	*113*
Leverage Emerging Innovations:	115
Loss of Purpose – (Why Am I Here …?)	116
Don't live to please somebody:	117
Don't Run the Rat Race:	118
Meet Your Real Self:	119
Meet the real you	*119*

Rediscover the enthusiasm of your childhood	*119*
Give something back:	*119*
Set your dreams on fire and keep them burning:	*120*
Honor God with your life:	*120*
Belief in God:	*120*
Dedication	**123**
Acknowledgment	**124**
What say my collegues and friends	**126**
Short Bio of Ishmeal Alfred Charles	**128**
Healey International Relief Foundation	**130**
Caritas Freetown	**132**
Sick Pikin Project	**134**